HISTORIC POTTSTOWN FAMILIES
in Stories and Photos

BEE JAY CALDWELL

Text copyright © 2016 Bee Jay Caldwell

All rights reserved. No part of this book may be reproduced or transmitted in any form or by any means, electronic or mechanical, including photocopying, recording, or by any information storage system, without permission in writing from the author.

The photos featured in this book are from the author's personal albums and / or were given to the author with permission from the featured individual. The stories were compiled by the author and were written from her perspective.

ISBN: 978-1-943258-29-1

Printed in the United States of America

Warren Publishing
3440 Toringdon Way, Suite 205
Charlotte, NC 28277

www.warrenpublishing.net

Dedication

To our beloved, blessed, segregated and enslaved ancestors who want to be acknowledged and remembered. They did not suffer those hardships for some one to say that their story is "folklore." Slave masters were just like bosses or supervisors; some were fair and some unfair. Others were down right cruel, mean and always on the attack.

The enslaved African in the American chattel slavery system is like the Egyptian pyramids. They both tell a story that cannot be disputed. The hands and feet, the blood and tears of these nameless heroes and sheroes were made to give America their best, including their lives. All this was done by people of privilege who demanded their freedom while denying people of color theirs.

Every nationality has been enslaved. None but the African could withstand the brutality of American chattel slavery. Because he survived hundreds of years of the horrors of slavery, he was ridiculed and demonized. In his heart, he was well aware that he was mistreated out of hatred and the desire for one race to feel superior to another. He believed that at some time in the future the Creator of the universe would right this manmade injustice and set their descendants free.

Our ancestors did so much more with so much less than what we have today. It was… It is… and forever shall be… "All about the love of God… and all about the love of family, and our fellowman / woman."

Because they were, *we are*!

TABLE OF CONTENTS

Introduction	6
No Place But the Quarters to Live	8
Christmas in the Slave Quarters	9
Becoming a Land Owner	10
Pay For Their Labor	13
Mini Family Biographies	14
The Barringer Brothers	14
Samuel Avon Barringer	14
Alex Henderson	14
William Kerns, Sr.	14
Reed and Esther Hicks	14
Espie Alexander	14
Randolph Grier	14
The Houston Brothers	15
Stanley Sloan, Sr.	15
Reverend S.B. Brown	15
Slyvester Springs	15
Rush Sherrill	15
John Kerns	15
Isaac Kerns	15
Fonzo Wilson	15
George Sutton	15
Clyde Neely	15
Lonnie Whitley	15
Albert Alexander, Sr.	15
Albert Alexander, Jr.	15
Edward "E" Smith	16
The Pharr Brothers	16
James "Teen" Patterson	16
Fred Douglas	16
Will Hughey	16
Sam Sloan	16
All Families Were Counted as Important and Vital	17
Young Married Families of 1954-1960	19
Getting an Education	20
Freedmen Schools	20
Segregation and Church Schools	20
Rosenwald Schools	20
Huntersville Colored School became Torrence-Lytle High School	20
Teachers	20
Leroy Wynn	20
F. M. Jones	20
Esther Johnson	20
Why the Pottstown Connection to Lytle Grove	21
Mighty Military Men of Pottstown	38
Sgt. David Alexander (WWII)	38
Spurgeon Caldwell (WWII)	38

- *Ulysses Grant (WWII)* 38
- *Ernest William (WWII)* 38
- *Joe Hicks (Korea-Vietnam)* 40
- *James Caldwell (Vietnam)* 40
- *Charlie Moore (Vietnam)* 40
- *Everette Houston* 40
- *Shawn Caldwell (Beirut)* 42

THEY GAVE THEIR LIVES 43
- *Lovette Sherrill, Daryl Clark and Walter Harris* 43

RELIGIOUS ACTIVITIES AND FUNCTIONS 48
- *Bethesda AME Zion Church's Annual Homecoming Picnic* 48

RECREATION AND ENTERTAINMENT 52
- *Camp Meetings and Picnics* 52
- *Music and the Juke Box* 52
- *Barringer and Berry's Place* 52
- *Dance Halls and the Do Drop In* 52
- *Beverages To Choose* 52

THE GREEN BOOK 53
- *Barber and Beauty Shops* 55
- *Snow Cones (Balls) and Pictures* 55
- *Take Us Out To The Ball Game* 55
- *Chris Springs* 55
- *Clyde Moore* 55

HALLOWEEN TRICKS (OR RIGHT OF PASSAGE) 53
- *Outdoor Toilets and Mr. Otha's Wagon* 53

THE DARK SIDE OF POTTSTOWN'S LIFE 53

HISTORY OF JUNETEENTH 66

IN RECOGNITION OF MY ANCESTORS BY BETTY JANE "BEE JAY" CALDWELL 67

MY STORY BEGAN ON THE WAY TO SCHOOL 70

EPILOGUE 97

INTRODUCTION

Historic Pottstown Families is envisioned as a tribute to the lives of Mr. and Mrs. Otha Potts and all those who lived and survived the horrors of slavery and the manmade Jim Crow laws, of separate but equal, with one problem: that separate was never equal.

It is written to be an inspiration to all who came after them to understand that "nothing just happens." There is a Master Plan and God orchestrates His Will.

These early Negroes knew that life would hand them trouble as they witnessed loved ones who had to go and loved ones who had to stay. They had a relationship with God and believed that one day, things would be changed. They believed that one day, God would use one person to change the rest of their lives as He did when Otha sold parcels of land to Negroes for the first time in the history of Huntersville.

Once and a while, individuals are born with a distinct destiny that proves to be a beacon for the dreams and hopes of many. Mr. and Mrs. Otha Potts knew the value of being landowners and wanted to share this opportunity with others. They proved their love for their fellowman by selling parcels to those who were sharecroppers or had lived in the former quarters.

There is no library for me to enter to research for a glimpse of the lives of the extraordinary people whose courage was renewed each day because they knew that the will of God would be worked out in their lives. These remembrances and recollections are gathered from seniors who had to search the corners of their minds 70, 80 and 90 years ago to tell their stories.

A debt of gratitude is owed to the late Mrs. Isabelle Hudson who passed away in 2014 at the age of 94. Many days the three of us, she, her nephew, Mr. Sam Barringer, and I set on her porch and shared the names of families living in Pottstown. Others who contributed to this story are, Mr. Parks Ross, Mrs. Emma Sloan, Mrs. Melissa Sherrill, Mrs. Barbara Kerns Smith, Mrs. Wilma Ladda and Ms. Pauline Caldwell.

Otha Potts (Patto) Biography

Otha Potts (whose last name was also written as Patto in one US Federal Census) was born in 1884 or 1885 in Wilkes County, North Carolina. His profession was a highly sought after brick mason and farmer. While living in Wilkes County, he was married. Later, he relocated to Mecklenburg County and purchased a large parcel of land outside of the city limits of Huntersville. In 1909, that governing body named the area where he lived "Pottstown" because he was a well-known, prominent citizen.

Those who knew him said that he was a quiet, soft-spoken man who trained other men in the area in the art of plastering and laying brick. He knew the value of being a land owner and also sold parcels of land to men with families.

In the early 1920s he married a nurse, Daisy McElrath. She was the daughter of Stanley McElrath who was a relative of one of the prominent "Lytle Men" living in "Lytle Grove," a predominant black community named for them in eastern Mecklenburg County.

Otha and Daisy made their home on a dirt road (now called Church Street) across the railroad tracks from the slave quarters in Huntersville. A few white families lived in homes already there. While they were getting water for drinking and washing from "springs," the Potts' home had a pump that they gladly allowed the neighbors to access. Their remains are buried at a Presbyterian Church in Huntersville.

The home they shared is still standing and is listed on the National Register of Historic Properties. Until a few years ago, the house was a rental home. There was a fire on the property and it is currently vacant.

No Place but the Quarters to Live
Segregation in a New Century

At the turn of the twentieth century, each town had an area designated for descendants of the "enslaved" called "the quarters." In Huntersville, this area was approximately one mile south of the town square at Gilead Road and HWY #115 and west of the railroad tracks in the vicinity of CPCC's North Campus.

East of HWY #115 and the railroad tracks was a large farm owned by a mulatto brick mason, Otha Potts and his wife. They were aware of the plight facing Negroes when it came to purchasing land and were willing to sell portions of theirs. As these descendants of slaves worked, became self-employed and made enough money to purchase land, Mr. Otha Potts gladly sold to them.

In 1909, the governing body of Huntersville designated the area where the Potts lived as an up-and-coming community for Negroes, even though white families were living there also. "Pottstown" was the name they gave to this new community.

Its purpose was never to function as a municipality. It was a designated place for designated people whose houses would be first generation homes of descendants of the enslaved Africans. During the 1960s, 70s and 80s, Federal block grants were obtained by Mecklenburg County to help the residents keep up their homes. In the past fifteen plus years that Pottstown has been in the town limits of Huntersville, any Federal grants obtained were used as incentives/perks to bring new entities to the business park that is adjacent (south) of the Pottstown community. Huntersville is home to over 55,000 white, Latino, Asian and black citizens.

In 2016, Pottstown looks almost as it did in 1909 as there are no sidewalks and there is no street infrastructure. All homes have inside running water and bathrooms but they are deteriorating. It is considered "prime property" and is in harm's way of being gentrified. This means the area is too good for working-class blacks, but just right for a developer to come and build modern, upscale homes that only individuals new to the area can afford.

Otha and Daisy Potts House, 2016 is on the National Register of Historic Properties

Christmas in the Slave Quarters

Before there was Pottstown, there were "The Quarters"

In the 1900s, the site of the slave quarters was one mile south of Huntersville located approximately where CPCC North campus is. The Quarters were usually located far enough from the whites who lived within the town, so as not to live in their eyesight, yet close enough for descendants of the enslaved to walk to their jobs in white homes.

The dwellings of those living in the quarters were one- or two- room shacks. Most did not have windows, just an opening with a wooden gate, like a door that could be closed and opened. Most did not have beds — the enslaved and their descendants slept on the dirt floor or in the loft on sacks filled with straw, called "ticks."

Early Christmas morning, the enslaved would go to the master's home and shout, "Christmas Give" and he would give each family member a gift. It was considered in very poor taste by other slave owners if the master did not give gifts to his enslaved population.

This was done for two reasons:
1. To keep them content and happy, so they wouldn't dwell on their powerlessness.
2. For the slave owner to show some humility to the enslaved and appease his conscience.

The master or slave owner did not allow his enslaved persons to drink liquor, but at Christmas he encouraged them to drink until they were drunk. Then he would insist that they follow his orders so that he could laugh at them.

The Yule Log was the height of the enslaved Christmas. As long as it burned at least twelve hours, the enslaved did not have to work. Usually one of the enslaved men would soak the log in water and then add brandy so that it would burn slow and long.

Becoming a Land Owner

Pottstown soon became the area that drew families whose only homes had been those in the quarters. Others were share croppers who knew how to farm, but did not own land. Finally after years of not having, these men and their families' dreams and hopes of being land owners came true.

Pillars of the Community

As years passed, Pottstown expanded to the "Bottom and Across the Hill." Families living in either section became pillars of the community:

- Albert Alexander, Sr., and wife, Flossie;
- Clyde Neely and wife, Viola
- Reed Hicks and wife, Esther
- Sylvester Springs and wife, Elizabeth
- Chris Springs and wife, Juanita
- Vicque Bryant, and wife, Rebecca
- James Trapp and wife, Peggy
- Robert Rivens and wife, Carrie
- Eugene Black and wife, Earlene
- Isaac Harris and wife, Alberta
- Cicero Black, and wife, Emma
- Harvey Haines and wife, Gertrude
- Fred Douglas and wife, Edna
- Charles Berry and wife, Lena
- Johnny Berry and wife, Lillie
- Albert Johnson and wife, Annie
- Frank Torrence and wife, Naomi

Among other Negro families to move to Pottstown was the Jasper Cleo Ross Family. Mr. Cleo was a farmer from Gaffney, South Carolina, a WWI survivor who rented homes to Negroes. He worked as a janitor and his wife, Ola was a nurse at the TB Sanitarium. Their children were Annie, L.C., twins, Louise and Lucinda, Margaret, Parks, John Henry and Roosevelt. As they grew up and learned that there was more to life than living and working on a farm, they moved to other states, seeking a better life for themselves. One son, Parks still lives in the home and a sister lives in Texas.

Elz Ross was Cleo's brother and a farmer. Soon he was living in Pottstown with his wife, Jennie Stinson. They had a large family. Their children were Kermit, Melvin, and Sidney Houston, Elz, Jr., Herman, Peggy, Mildred, Zora, Thelma, Walter and Raymond Ross.

Another set of brothers moved into Pottstown: the Grier's — Randolph, Frances and Leroy were self-employed carpenters and plasters.

Dellwood Drive in 2016

Church Street in 2016

Corner of Holbrooks Road and Haven Drive in 2016

Central Avenue in 2016

Pay For Their Labor

The TB Sanitarium was an employing destination for Negroes from its opening in the 1920s to the year 2000. These men or women were assured a job on the "Ward" or in the kitchen. If you were from out of town, you could stay on "the lot" in the boys or nursing home. Sylvester Springs, Charles Berry, Vicque Bryant, Eugene Black, Fred Douglas, Spurgeon Caldwell, Frank Sloan and Louis Barringer worked there. Some of the women who worked there were Pearl Turner, Ola Ross, Hazelene Harris, Shirley Greer, Hallie Patterson, Shirley Caldwell, Mamie Kerns, Elizabeth Springs, Alice Allison, Barbara Smith, Helen Trapp, Lora Thompson, Arlene Alexander, Emma Sloan, Mary Sherrill, Anna Barringer, Melissa Sherrill, and Evelyn Barringer.

Negro men needed to move beyond farming, to be self-employed or work almost for free. The following men found good paying jobs.

Isaac Harris, Murray Neal and Ciscero Black worked for the railroad.

Troy Barringer, Lawrence Caldwell and Reed Hicks worked at the cotton mill in Huntersville and Clyde Neeley worked for the cotton mill in Cornelius.

James Trapp and Bud Marr were janitors at Huntersville's Colored School.

Tom Johnson worked for the town of Huntersville.

Spurgeon Caldwell worked for a union trucking company, Trail-mobile.

William "June" Kerns worked in Charlotte and cut hair at home.

Isaac B. Thompson, Cooder Ramseur, Bus Wilson and Craven Stinson were plasterers.

Stanley Sloan was a brick mason.

Frank Torrence was a painter.

Sam Berry was a carpenter.

Mini Family Biographies

The melodious voices of the **Barringer brothers** filled the rural airways of Pottstown and Mecklenburg County with spiritual music. Curlee, Leroy, James, Fred, Louis, Troy, Wilber, and sisters, Rebecca and Isabelle were musically inclined entrepreneurs who formed a singing group that performed throughout local counties. Curlee was married to a teacher, **Anna Grier**, who just passed away in 2015 at 98 years old. They were parents to Jerome, Delores, Gloria, James, Madelyn, Debbie and Clement. Brother Fred was married to Vestula and Troy was married to Wealthy.

Samuel Avon Barringer shared most of the stories from the era before I was born. He is the oldest son of **Doretha Rebecca Barringer** and has a younger brother, Joseph. His first grade teacher at Huntersville's Rosenwald School was Mrs. Haley. He sang in the glee club at Huntersville Colored School and sings in the male chorus at his church. He obtained his first job at Johnson Mills when he was sixteen years old. He learned to work on cars out of necessity and never married. He is retired now, and remembers that "A black man did not have a chance at nothing and whites did not have too much either."

Self-employed plasterer, **Alex Henderson**, was husband to Frankie, father to Ruby, and grandfather to Twanna and Hawiatha Nivens. He was also a savvy businessman, whose skills were often sought after by whites to help build their homes. He had lived in large cities and had a better vision for the future of Pottstown. In the late 1940s after WWII, Pottstown's citizens were still getting wash and drinking water from the springs. He observed this and wanted to do something to change it. He approached Huntersville's governing body and requested their assistance. What he eventually got was their permission to buy the pipe and to dig the trench to supply water to Pottstown. As a result, he organized the men, purchased the galvanized water line pipe from a former military camp and used their hands to dig the trench on Dellwood Drive and Central Avenue to bring families running water.

William Kerns, Sr., and wife, **Mamie Turner**, were entrepreneurs who lived out their lives in Pottstown. They were parents to Barbara, Hazel, Bernice (died as an infant,) Pearl, William, Carolyn and Diane.

Reed and **Esther Hicks** were parents to Joe Gene, Maggie, Andrew, Donald and Cecil. Mr. Reed was employed at the mill in Huntersville. Maggie graduated from Huntersville Colored High School. She was mother to Paul and Cathy. An older sister moved to Washington, DC. Paul passed away this year and was known throughout Mecklenburg County for his ability to sing for the Lord.

Espie Alexander and his wife, **Viola**, lived next door to the Rosenwald School, affectionately called, the "Little School." Every morning he would make a fire in each of the four classrooms so that they would be warm when the students arrived.

Randolph Grier was married to **Alberta** and lived in front of the school. They had a large family, Louise, Mary, Rosetta, Hubert, J. D. "Slackie," Lonnie, Joyce, Beatrice, Randolph Jr., Herman, Otis, Joe and Priscilla. Randolph, Sr., his sons, and nephews were members of the United House of Prayer (UHOP). In the 1970s, 1980s, and 1990s these men rose to fame by building United House of Prayers throughout the United States.

The **Houston brothers**, Eugene, Hubert, Buddy, and Luther were skilled cement finishers who only completed grade school but could lay concrete better, and with less waste than those who had college degrees. Eugene was married to Irene and they had two sons, Cooda and Eugene. Hubert "Hub" was married to Mrs. Will and they rented homes to Negroes. Buddy was married to Cora and they had several children, James, Alfred, Lee Andy, Sarah, Betty, Joanne, and Zette. Luther was married to Geneva and they had a daughter, Dorothy.

Stanley Sloan, Sr. was married to **Emma Gaston** who is still alive today at over 90 years old. Their daughters, Betty, Geraldine, and Mary continue to provide care for her. Joanne and Stanley, Jr. are deceased.

Reverend S. B. Brown, a son of the community, and his wife, **Laura,** were Pastor and first lady at Chapel Hill Missionary Baptist Church. They were parents of Mary Ann, Sarah, Sylvester, Helen and a younger sister.

Sylvester Springs and his wife, **Elizabeth,** and their sons: Garland, Larry, Jerry, Billy and daughter, Dorothy lived in Pottstown. They were the first family I ever met that was not related to me. Garland and I entered first grade together, graduated in 1964 and became pen pals while he was in the Air Force.

The Sherrills, Rush and wife, **Mary** moved into a home that was already on Church Street. He was employed at an appliance store. They had several children, Annie, Doris, Rush, Jr., Gwendolyn, Beverlyn and Terry. Soon they opened the community grocery store, "Sherrill's Grocery."

John Kerns, and wife, **Mary Jane,** lived west of the railroad tracks with their two daughters, Johnsie and Gerthie Mae. As Negro women obtained jobs outside their homes, Ms. Mae Jane became a "loving" community babysitter.

Isaac Kerns lived in Pottstown and bought a house on the corner of Holbrooks Road and Church Street.

Fonzo Wilson and his wife, **Susie,** lived on what is now Central Avenue. He was employed at a prison where the men worked on "a chain gang."

George Sutton, and his wife, **Gertrude Haines,** had one daughter, Catherine, and lived by the railroad tracks and "Little Mission" (Huntersville AME Zion Church).

Clyde Neely lived in Cornelius before he moved to Pottstown. His wife died and he married Viola. Her grandsons, Bus and Wardell Wilson lived with them. A daughter or relative, named Janie, from Neck Road lived there also.

Lonnie Whitley and his wife, **Kizzie Gibson,** had several children. Deanie, Dorothy, Annie, Sister Bill, Matthew, Lona, Millie, Dank, Dave, Gene, Edna, Susie and Betty. They lived below the Mill Hill in Huntersville.

Gilbert Calvin "GC" Moultry and wife, **Ruth Alberta,** had a large family and were parents to Annie Lee Holman, Calvin, Lester, James Odell, Odessa, Artis, Fred, Bobby, Mable, Connie, Donnie, Gene, Glenn, Claude and Frances. Many members of this fine family still live in the area.

Albert Alexander, Sr. and wife, **Flossie** lived at the top of the hill. Their daughters were, Catherine, Emma, Bobbie Jean, Rebecca and Carol. Their sons are Albert, Jr., James, Frank and Ronnie.

Albert Alexander, Jr., was married for over fifty years to **Arlene Whitley,** who just passed away in August of 2016. My first job as babysitter was to keep their oldest sons, George, Robert and sometimes cousin, "Little Beaver." Later on I babysat for their other children, Diane, Phyllis, Waddell and Big Eye.

Cement finisher, **Edward** or "E. Smith" and wife, **Ruth Caldwell**, raised their family in Pottstown. They were parents to James, Pee Wee, Johnsie, Roberta, Wayne, T-Bo, Bobbie, Fern, and twin girls, Ruth Alfreda and Felix Smith.

The **Pharr brothers,** Baxter and Henry of Pottstown had ties to the Pharr's of Long Creek. Baxter was married to Ella Faye Howard. She was instrumental in having a lighted tree on the corner of Central Avenue and Holbrooks Road at Christmas. Henry was married to Liza. His position as night watchman at the hospital was very important to the safety of the institution as he carried a gun and a lantern.

James "Teen" Patterson and his wife, **Hallie,** moved to Pottstown from Mallard Creek. Their sons, Louis, Larry and Mack are avid outdoorsmen who love to fish and hunt. Their daughters, Drucilla, Linda and Josie are good cooks like their mother. Twins, Larry and Linda were born and Hallie's twin sisters lived with them.

Fred and **Edna Douglas** were another couple with a large family. They were parents to Fred, Jr., Dorothy Belle, Mary, William, Luke, Melvin, Alice, Charles, Harry, Jo Lillian and Angela.

In the early 1960s, the **Will** and **Annie Blaire Hughey** family moved to Pottstown. They had several children, Moses and another son died leaving Fred James, Ethel Mae, Earlene, Robert, Johnny, Geraldine and Carolyn.

Cement finisher, **Sam Sloan** and his wife, **Lula Belle** lived in Pottstown and sometimes in different places in Huntersville. Their family included several children.

ALL FAMILIES WERE COUNTED AS IMPORTANT AND VITAL

Even though most families consisted of a husband, wife and children, there were other families that did not.

Mr. Dee Alexander was Little David's father. He liked flowers and they grew around the path to his front door and surrounded his house. Twin trees stood at the street welcoming everyone in. To me and my friends, it looked like the houses shown in fairy tales.

Bill Currance's wife died and he worked in Charlotte.

Sisters or cousins, Carrie and Hazeline lived together with Hazeline's son, Tommy Gene.

Cora Fletcher's husband, John, died and she reared their sons, Marshall (Duke), and Terry, and two daughters, Doris and Pattie.

"Bubble Up" Allison lived with his relative, Odessa Staton.

Ciscero Black, a widower, had two daughters, "Sing" and "Sang."

Catherine Alexander Brown was married and has a son, Wayne, and two daughters, Deborah and Myra. For years she was president of HCDA.

Pearl McClelland lived with her son, Donald Ray.

Etta Connor had two sons, Harry Connor and James Lynch.

Harry Connor his wife, Teretha, and children, Mary, Harry Jr., Dorothy and Jean, lived in Pottstown and sometimes in the city limits of Huntersville.

James Lynch was married to Ossie Lee Lynch and they had a family.

Rovenia McKinley's husband died and she lived with her adult children, Mary, Sonny, Sister Bill, Martha, and twins, Robert and Minnie.

Lonnie Berry and wife, Minnie; Harvey Haines and wife, Gertrude; and Jim Neal and wife, Flora, lived near Dwight Cross' air plane hanger (located where the Huntersville Business Park is now).

Earle Clark and Pete Clark (not related) lived in the Bottom.

Nettie Davis' husband drowned in Lake Norman. She and their son, Freddie and daughter were relatives of "Mac Doodle" Davis.

Three Gaston brothers lived in Pottstown, Claude, Harry and John.

Harry Gaston and wife, Bertha, and their three daughters, Cora, Doris, and Wilma owned property in the Bottom.

Frank Harris and wife, Maggie, and their children lived in Gibson Park.

Minnie Gibson, widow of Albert Gibson, and two of their sons, Andrew and Paul Faith lived in Pottstown. Paul married Elaine Moore, became a minister and was an associate pastor at Chapel Hill Baptist Church. They have two sons, Joe and Will.

Daisy Mae Trapp Moore was a neighbor of Little Mission Church. She would host some of those fun-filled summer picnics. Her daughter, Sarah and one of her sons, David, still reside there.

Hattie Allison, a widow, moved to Pottstown from the Lytle Grove area. She had children and two of them, Raymond and Johnsie were teachers.

Bert Harris and wife, Hattie lived near Isaac Harris and wife, Alberta.

The names of individuals listed below lived in Pottstown. Information about them has been lost in the memories of those who have passed on.

Murray Neal, Cleveland Caldwell, Maggie Whitley, John Moore, Ernest Trapp, Johnnie Mae Harris, Bessie Holman, Celebo Houston, Buddy Trapp, Mazon and Mattie Sherrill, Will and Cat Alexander, Bub and Louise Stowe, John and Massie Vannon Whitley and John and Virginia Morrison Little.

- Austin Pharr, his daughter, **Ida Howard,** and her family, sons, **James** and **Gabby** and daughters, **Rose Anne** and **Bettye** came from Long Creek.
- **John Johnson** and wife, **Christine** were related to **Maggie Johnson**.
- **Vicque** and **Rebecca Bryant's** son, **Harvey** and his wife, have been in the funeral home business as a mortician and undertaker for over fifty years.
- Time has removed from our memories the name of the mother of the Whitley brothers and sisters who were **Thomas, Dickie, Sam, "Sun Whit," Odis (Peanut), Odessa, Maggie, Susie Mae, Edna** and **Arlene**. Each lived out a full life in the Pottstown area.
- In their young years, **John Caldwell** was married to **Sarah Jetton**. They were parents to **Lawrence Wayne, Gail, Brian, Donna** and **Allen**.
- **Clarence Lynch** and wife, **Bernice,** were related to siblings, **LeMont** and **Hazeline Lynch**.
- **Calvin Morrison** and wife, **Nancy** were parents of **Claudie Morrison** who had a wife, **Mildred,** and children.
- **Roxie Potts** was **Hattie, Tom** and **Will "Rocks'"** mother and grandmother to **William** and daughters **Betty**, and **Annie Lit**.
- **Frank Sloan,** Stanley's brother, had two sons, **Jake** and **Ernest**.
- **Ernest Springs** was a widower, and had a large family whose names are lost to time.
- **Charles Little** had four married sisters living in Pottstown, **Alberta Grier, Willett Houston, Viola Neely** and **Rena Lucky**.
- **Mary Lou Alexander** lived with her son, **Johnny** and daughter, **Barbara Anne**.
- **Minnie Montieth,** her son, **Bill,** and daughter, **Berdie Lee,** lived across HWY #115, west of Pottstown, on the property of the white Montieths.
- **Isaac B. Thompson** and wife, **Helen** and sons, **Wayne, Vernon** and **Greg** built a home on Church Street.
- **Lorenza Graham (Billie Hicks)** her mother, **Flossie,** and son, **Reginald,** built a home on Church Street.
- **Alexander Moore** and wife, **Lola,** had three adult sons, **Lewis, Sam** and **Clyde.** They built a home on Church Street.
- **Odis Whitley** and wife, **Marie,** built a home on Church Street for **Denny, Darnell, Jerry, Pam,** and another son and daughter.
- **Delores "Dee" Springs** lived on Central Avenue with her three sons.
- **Mr. Hudson,** in the winter, would cut steps into the hillside so residents could find their way down the hill to get safely across.
- **Alex Trapp,** wife **Helen,** and their family lived near other family members.
- Siblings, **Haywood, Allen** and **Danette Allison** lived in the Bottom with their mother, **Alice** after their dad, **Luke** passed away.
- **Mr. Lonnie Berry** and his wife, **Lillie** lived on Holbrooks Road. Their home was moved to Church Street to make room for an addition to the school. They had a daughter, Louise, who lived in Washington, DC. They reared a relative's daughter named Edna Mae. Mrs. Lillie was the eyes and ears of Church Street and gave neighborhood children muffins.

Young Married Families of 1954 – 1960

Albert and Arlene Whitley Alexander
Pete and Barbara Johnson Alexander
Will and Cat Alexander
Sam and Mary Ella Graham Berry
Donald and Annie Potts Beatty
Sylvester and Geraldine Sloan Brown
Peter, Jr. and Betty Barringer Clark
Arthur and Mary McKinley Davis
William and Edna Mae Berry Douglas
Hurbert and Victoria Thompson Grier
Walter and Justine Springs Hall
Eugene and Iretha Long Houston
James "Bo" and Shirley Caldwell Howard
Robert and Johnsie Smith Hughey
James and Mildred "Millie" Whitley Jackson
Jerry and Joanne Sloan Johnson
Leon and Wilma Gaston Ladda
James and Ossie Lee Lynch
Clyde and Betty Howard Moore
Lewis and Ethel Mae Hughey Moore
Lester and Earlene Hughey Moultry
Raymond and Betty Sloan Phillips
Johnny Ed and Dorothy Bell Douglas Relliford
Elz and Lucy Berry Ross
Mot "Gus" and Christine McDowell Sherrill
Isaac and Melissa Berry Sherrill
Roland and Mary Connor Sherrill
Jake and Lona Whitley Sloan
Charles and Dorothy Houston Smith
Ferman and Barbara Kerns Smith
Charles and Bobbie Jean Alexander Springs
James and Mary Davis Staton
Clarence and Betty Davis Staton
Ward and Odessa Whitley Staton
Zeek and Minnie McKinley Thompson
Isaac and Rosetta Grier White
Odis and Marie Burton Whitley

Other families consisted of single mothers, Maggie Hicks, Rose Anne Howard, Martha McKinley, Mae Travis Sherrill and Lula Belle Springs. Odessa Whitley Staton helped rear her nephews, George, Robert and "Little Beaver."

Getting an Education

Teachers

The descendents of slaves knew the importance and value of getting an education even though there were no public schools for Negroes. Freedmen would build a school in communities where a large number lived. Students came from throughout Mecklenburg County to attend the little three room schoolhouse built at the corner of Eastfield and Alexandriana Roads about three miles from the town square in a section called "Joppa." Thanks to God, it was not demolished to make room for I-485. In 2014, it was relocated to Rural Hill in western Mecklenburg County where it hopefully will be restored.

During the days of segregation, schools and churches were the main places Negroes could meet in the rural South because of the laws of the USA.

Local churches opened their doors for Negroes to secure a much desired education. Miranda School was located on Miranda Road in Charlotte on the grounds of Miranda Presbyterian Church. In the 1950s the church merged with Caldwell Presbyterian Church located on HWY #73 in Huntersville and formed Catawba Presbyterian Church located on McCoy Road in Huntersville. The Miranda School house was relocated on the grounds of Catawba Presbyterian Church. It is still there today. Chapel Hill Missionary Baptist Church located on Mt. Holly-Huntersville Road operated its school in the early 1920s as did Pleasant Grove Church.

In 1913, Julius Rosenwald was president of Sears/Roebuck Company. He wanted to improve the educational opportunities for Negroes in the south. He partnered with Booker T. Washington of Tuskegee Institute to build what became known as the Rosenwald 1, 2, 3, 4, and 5 room school houses. They contained grades one through six. Mr. Rosenwald provided the funds that had to be matched by the community and Mr. Washington provided the architectural drawings for each. Families wanting a school in their community worked hard to obtain the two or three thousand dollars it took to match these funds. Over the years, 5,300 Rosenwald school buildings were built in fifteen southern states. Lytle Grove Rosenwald School was built at Columbus Chapel Church but was destroyed by fire. Huntersville had one located on Dellwood Drive but lost its designation because the windows were altered.

In the 1930s, there was not a high school in the northern end of Mecklenburg County for Negroes. If a student living there wanted to secure an education beyond the sixth grade, he/she would have to attend boarding school. Two prominent men, Mr. Isaiah Torrence and Mr. Frank Lytle, born a slave, lobbied the Mecklenburg County Commissioners for a school. With Mr. Lytle donating the land, in 1937 Huntersville Colored School was completed and ready to receive students in grades seven through eleven. The opening of this long awaited high school was *welcomed* with open arms by all Negro families in northern Mecklenburg County. This also meant that new teachers would be hired and some eventually came to live within the Pottstown community. Its one and only principal, Mr. Isaac T. Graham, served from 1937 until 1966.

One of the teachers, Leroy Wynn and his wife, Levera, lived out their lives in Pottstown. After Huntersville Colored School (Torrence-Lytle) closed, Mr. Wynn worked and retired from North Mecklenburg High School. Two of their daughters, Verona and Cassandra, still reside here. Mr. F. M Jones, his wife and son resided in Pottstown until the school closed. He was employed with Charlotte-Mecklenburg School System at Second Ward High School. Mrs. Esther Stinson Johnson, English teacher and librarian, came to the school one year after it opened. She retired as librarian from Huntersville Elementary School. Her family owned land in western Huntersville near the Catawba River.

These teachers, along with others who were hired, became "role model icons" to the students who attended the newly re-named Torrence-Lytle High School in 1953-54. These students came from Charlotte, Derita, Long Creek, Mallard Creek, Cornelius, Davidson, and of course Huntersville. Several living in small Mecklenburg County communities, i.e. Columbus Chapel/Lytle Grove, Gibson Park, and Ritch Hatchett Road also attended. To them the opportunity of a lifetime was being able to attend high school in their home town instead of attending boarding school in another county.

Why the Pottstown Connection To Lytle Grove

After the Civil War, Huntersville had no sub-divisions and there was no way to identify where you lived. As was the practice before the war, white families continued to name their homesteads, (i.e. Latta or Holly Bend Plantations) this made it easier for them to be located. That is why communities of well-to-do descendants of the enslaved had to have names, hence, Pottstown and Lytle Grove.

European fathers of enslaved Africans who had taught them to read and write also allocated land to them. Upon a first glance of these individuals, one could hardly distinguish them from the Europeans. In the days of slavery, they were house servants or artisans (men or women with specific skills: blacksmiths, midwives, and preachers who became teachers). As was the practice of their Masters, these well-to-do men, with good character, became community leaders. And to distinguish where they lived in east Huntersville, the name "Lytle Grove" was given to the large parcels of land they owned on Huntersville Concord Road.

One such family living in there was the Lytles, of whom Mrs. Daisy McElrath Potts was a descendant. Mrs. Ophelia Lytle Alexander, the daughter of Susie Mae Whitley, and step daughter of Will Lytle, shares her recollections of the Lytle family.

As a high school student at Huntersville Colored School, before the days of caregivers/companions who helped seniors remain at their homes, Ophelia provided in-home assistance to Mrs. Daisy Potts' parents. She called them "Grandpa Stanley" and "Granny Ida." Growing up in their midst, she has first-hand knowledge of the closeness of the Lytle and Potts families.

Now a senior herself, she recollects that Old man Frank Lytle and his wife, Lizzie lived in a large two story home, on several acres of land on Huntersville Concord Road. Other Lytle family members owned large adjourning tracks of land. Teachers Eva and Liza lived nearby and taught at Columbus Chapel's Rosenwald School. Mrs. Daisy had two sisters, Bessie and Carrie, and two brothers, Milas and John. Carrie married Julius Lytle and gave Mrs. Daisy nephews, Bernizer, Will, John Stanley, Oscar and Alfonzo. They were very close to her and visited her and Mr. Otha at their Pottstown home. Nieces who moved away were Bessie, Sadie and Bernice. The Pottstown and Lytle Grove connection is not as strong as it once was, but a remnant will always remain as long as there are Lytle descendants present in Pottstown.

Mr. Isaac Torrence Graham, Sr.
Torrence-Lytle's One and Only Principal

As an educator, I.T. Graham remained a dedicated principal of Torrence-Lytle High School for 30 years, where he shed a great influence on students and community alike.

He was instrumental in eliminating the split school term for Blacks and securing a gymnasium and cafeteria for the black high school in his county.

Ike's accomplishments as a community leader included: a highly esteemed Ruling Elder in the Catawba Presbyterian Church and in the Catawba Presbytery; a charter member of the choir; and clerk of the session for over 15 years. He was instrumental in bringing the Risk Evangelism Program to this church, and served as a Resource Person for this area.

His untiring and fruitful services were stabilizing factors in the progress of this church. Ike initiated the successful merger of the Caldwell and Miranda churches — now Catawba Church. He worked in the same capacity attempting to bring together Huntersville, Davidson and Catawba churches into merger possibilities.

In his final work, he was instrumental in the movement of Catawba Presbytery to withdraw from Catawba Administrative Unit.

Other affiliations included: Chairman of the Mission Division of the Catawba Presbytery; Member of the Nominating Committee of the Synod of the Piedmont; Vice Moderator of Catawba Presbytery; and still other affiliations included: civic, social and political affairs.

"His life will not be a passing memory to those he taught and worked with on Earth, but will be a living monument to all who knew his worth."

Submitted by:
Carrie G. Potts
John C. and Byrd Graham

Torrence-Lytle's original 1937 building

Assembly Program in the 1940s

Huntersville Rosenwald School

Old TLHS

C. Dewitte Bradford Gym Waymer

Teachers at Huntersville Colored School

Former TLHS teachers, left to right, Juanita White and friend; student, Bo Carr; Nannie Rae Potts and Mae Burns Orr

Former librarian, Esther Stinson Johnson

My first grade teacher, Mrs. Streater, Mrs. Hunt and Ms. O.L. Brown

Mrs. J.P. White and student, Rush Sherrill

Mrs. J.P. White at class reunion

Elizabeth Adams Thompson Class of 1954

Elizabeth Adams Thompson Class of 1958

TLHS graduating class with principal, Mr. T. Graham and Mrs. Esther Stinson Johnson

Queens Bernice Walker and Evelyn Berry at TLHS 1960 May Day Celebration

TLHS 6th grade teacher, Emma Jean Saunders, goes to Washington, DC and Linville Caverns, 1959

TLHS Rhythm Band in 1958 with the music teacher and Mrs. B.K. Watkins

TLHS Dramatics Club 1958

1965 Head Start Class with teacher Ms. Beatrice McCollough

1960 TLHS Homecoming hosted by Davidson College. Homecoming queens were: Vivian White and Pauline Caldwell.

1964 classmates, front row, left to right Alice Douglas Reed, Betty Lowery Davis, Jimmy Brandon. Second row, left to right, Pearl Kerns Knox, Jimmy Knox, Annie Beatty Allison, Allen Allison, Betty Caldwell and Bernice Anderson

Cousins, Betty and Pearl at their 1964 graduation

In 2005, Betty Caldwell and Maggie Hicks make a public stand against demolishing TLHS

COMMUNITY LEADERS TOURED TLHS GRAMMAR CLASSROOMS

Community mothers, Emma Sloan and Mary Sherrill

Minnie Thompson, Rev. Davis, Emma Sloan, Nate Bowman (white shirt)

Saving TLHS in 2005, we were able to tour the grammar classrooms

Emma Sloan and Nate Bowmon

Mary Sherrill, Minnie Thompson, Madelyn Barringer and Gloria Elliott

Inside the grammar grade class building with Rev. Byrum Davis, Emma Sloan and Nate Bowman

Waymer Center Renovation

Estimate Cost for Repair - Design - Construction

1. Hazardous Materials

Item	Amount	Subtotal
Abatement Design, submittals and Bidding	4,500	
Asbestos Abatement (both friable and non friable)	77,800	
Air Monitoring, clearance sampling and Testing	17,000	
Abatement Subtotal		**99,300**

2. Construction Cost

Site

Site improvements, (railings, sidewalks, ADA)	15,000
Asphalt paving in rear for accessible parking & driveway (1,490 sy x $20/sy)	29,800
Fence relocation and repair	7,500
Landscape Maintenance	4,500

Gym Building

Building Roof (replace roof, gutters and downspouts)	265,000
Replace vinyl tile	10,200
Bleacher Replacement (including ADA Upgrade)	45,000
Demolition and Replacement of Gym wood floor (demo @ $3.00/sf, new @ $15/SF)	140,400
Painting (interior partitions, all doors, frames and exposed ceilings	45,500
Doors & Hardware (replace doors and hardware, use existing frames)	15,000
Windows/Glass (replace all windows and frames, new aluminum storefront at entrance	95,000
Repair plaster ceilings (water damaged plaster)	18,000
Mechanical - (replace all three units, 2 small & large gym)	131,000
Plumbing (replace fixtures, faucets, flush valve toilets and water heater, repair toilet partitions, 4 toilets)	22,000
Toilet Addition/Renovations for ADA (2 toilet rooms)	21,000
Electrical (replace service to building, new panels, light fixtures, switches, receptacles)	130,000
Fire Alarm (New)($3.00 SF)	51,000

Rear Wing

Item	Amount	Subtotal
Partial demolition of rear wing (windows, doors, non-load bearing walls, etc.)	15,000	
Repair/renovation to create open air covered area (roof replacement, exterior lighting, floor patching ,etc.)	40,000	
Construction Subtotal		**1,100,900**

3. Architect/Engineer Fees

Item	Amount	Subtotal
Estimated at 10% of estimated construction cost	110,090	110,090

Fees for Design, Bidding and Construction Administration Services for architecture, mechanical, plumbing, fire protection and electrical engineers.

Miscellaneous Expenses

#	Item	Amount	Subtotal
4	FF&E for Gym (6-tables and 48-chairs)	6,000	
5	OPE (Picnic tables 6 @ 1500 ea., Grill, @ 550, Scoreboard $25K ea.)	34,500	
4	Administrative Cost (advertisements, printing, etc.) (0.5%)	5,505	
	Permit and Regulatory Fees (1.5%)	16,514	
	Builders Risk Insurance	2,450	
	Miscellaneous Expense Subtotal	64,968	64,968

	Amount
Estimated Cost	1,375,258
Project Contingency (15% of Estimated Construction Cost)	165,135
Total Estimated Cost	**1,540,393**

1. Abatement cost were developed by S&ME and Allied Contract Group utilizing data obtained from hazardous materials inspection conducted on 3 Sept 2015.
2. The cost were estimated by facility assessment conducted by AFM-FMO in June 2014, local contractor input and site visits in Sept 2015.
3 & 4. These cost are historical data cost from past AFM projects.
5. Historical cost from other Park & Rec projects

3-Dec-2015   Prepared by Mecklenburg County Asset & Facility Management

Timeline for Restoration of Waymer Gym.

December 2015, Huntersville Town Building Meeting where the county commissioners were present and committed to restoring the gym to its original condition.

MIGHTY MILITARY MEN OF POTTSTOWN

Over one hundred men and women entered the armed forces from this small rural community in Huntersville in WWI, WWII, the Korean Conflict, Vietnam, Beirut, Desert Storm and in peace time. Pottstown men, who were treated as second class citizens, wanted to prove to the world that they loved their country, and would join the military to risk their lives for her.

Never shall we forget WWII Army medic, Sgt. David Alexander and nicknamed, "The Kingfish." He was a Pottstown's native who served in the Pacific Theater after having spent 32 days on a ship with 800 crew members and ten thousand men and women. The ship was so crowded that he had to sleep on the steps. The ship's first stop was Melbourne, Australia. Then it was on to the New Caledonian Islands, and the last stops were at Papua, New Guinea and Dutch, New Guinea. He saw a lot of combat and was honorably discharged from the Army, but the Army never left him. He became a recluse. He was always kind to us "chaps" (term used for children at that time) as we marched behind him as he sang the cadence of the Army's theme song. He often shared with us stories of how the German prisoners of war were treated better than the Negroes. Life has a way of correcting wrongs in the lives of some. This was the case of our beloved, "Little David." He was buried in the Veterans' Cemetery in Salisbury right next to the sidewalk where all who pass by can read his grave marker that says, "Sgt. D. Alexander, The Kingfish."

Spurgeon Caldwell relocated from Cornelius to work at the TB hospital where he met and married Shirley Johnson. Their children are James, Betty and Pauline. Their oldest daughter, Shirley, is deceased and was the mother of the "Bug Heads," Avery, Nette and Terry. He joined the Army, served in the European Theater as one of the Red Ball truck drivers. Once when he was driving over a bridge, it was hit by heavy enemy fire. He was thrown into a river and was rescued. After getting out of the Army, he went to school on the GI Bill, learned to lay brick and was paid to farm cotton. His brothers, James and Craven, served in WWII also, and his younger brother, Clifford, in the Korean Conflict.

Ulysses Grant and his wife, Onita relocated to Pottstown after he completed a stint in the Army in WWII. He received extensive training at Camp Robert Smalls in the use of explosives. He was a man of many professions. He grew animals and collected specimens for pharmaceutical laboratories. He worked as a watch repairman, a meat cutter, a brick mason, a carpenter and an auto mechanic. His nephew, Marion, joined the Air Force and was a jet mechanic who flew missions with the plane he was assigned while stationed in Vietnam.

Ernest Williams was married to Gertrude, was drafted during WWII and served as a member of the Quartermasters Corps. He landed on the beaches of Normandy two days after D-Day. While on guard duty one night, he captured four German soldiers by bluffing them. He heard rustling in the Quartermaster closet, and said in a loud voice, "I have a weapon. Come out!" Much to his surprise, four German soldiers surrendered. He received two Bronze star metals for the capture.

Other Pottstown men serving in WWII were James "McGoo" Barringer, Sam Berry, Pete Huntley, John Kerns and Rush Sherrill.

David Alexander, a WWII medic and Tamasheika Baker

WWII veteran Ulysses Grant trained at Camp Robert Smalls

TLHS 1964 graduate, and cousin Pearl's husband, Jimmy Knox joined the Army

TLHS 1961 graduate, James Caldwell, joined the Air Force

TLHS 1962 graduate, Stanley Sloan, Jr., joined the Army

Korea and Vietnam

Joe G. Hicks made a career of the Army. He was one of six children born to Mr. Reed and Mrs. Esther Hicks. He graduated from Torrence-Lytle High School in 1953 and entered the Army in 1954. He was trained at Fort Jackson, SC and his first duty station was Japan. He spent three years stateside then to Anchorage, Alaska then back to the contiguous United States. Next he was off to Korea. As an 11c40 Heavy Weapons Infantry Petroleum Specialist, he was off to Vietnam. He stayed in the Army so that his brothers would not have to go. He possessed a strong determination, and could say emphatically, without hesitation or reservation, "I could handle things." In all, he spent four years and six months in active duty in Vietnam. He was honorably discharged and returned to Pottstown where he shared his fascinating history with me, Bee Jay Caldwell.

Other Pottstown natives who served in the era of the Korean Conflict are:

- Rufus Blackmon
- John W. Clark, Jr.
- Ken Davis
- William Holman
- Kermit Houston
- Melvin Houston
- Sidney Houston
- Brother Johnson
- Tommy Johnson
- John Little
- Louis Moore
- Willie Nixon
- Baxter Pharr, Jr.
- Barney Ramsey
- James Staton
- Ward Staton
- Ralph Tucker
- Thomas Whitley, Sr.
- Dickie Whitley

Vietnam

James M. F. Caldwell graduated from Torrence-Lytle High School and spent a year and a half at A & T College before joining the Air Force the first day of spring in 1963. "The Air Force," in his own words, "is my first love." He had several duty stations after basic training in Texas: California, England, Texas, South Carolina, North Carolina and served two tours of duty in Vietnam. He retired after twenty years and became a state correctional officer. He is married to Annie Dargen of Goldsboro. James and Annie are parents to Tony and Duke University Graduate, April. His oldest daughter, Montez, gave him two grandsons, Adrian and Marcus and granddaughter, Tomeka.

Charlie Moore served honorably in the Army for over twenty years. He and his wife, Conella and family lived overseas for years. His last duty station was at the Pentagon in Washington, DC.

Everett Houston graduated from North Mecklenburg High School and joined the Army. He says, "Having successfully completed this period of rigorous training, I proved to be physically fit, knowledgeable in military subjects and qualified with my basic weapon. The value of this training can be measured only in terms of how I use the knowledge and skills I have acquired." He and his sons live in New Haven Park/Pottstown.

Uncle Clifford Caldwell fought in the Korean Conflict.

1964 Torrence-Lytle High School graduate Garland Springs, joined the Air Force.

Cousins joined the military, left, William Kerns, Jr. and Bernard Houston

Army, Aaron Smith

Marine, Shawn Caldwell

Beirut

Shawn Caldwell is a graduate of North Mecklenburg High School. Soon after graduation, he walked into the Marine's recruiting office and enlisted. A few days later, he was in "Boot Camp" fighting sand fleas at Parris Island, South Carolina. In 1983 the BLT was bombed in Beirut, Lebanon. He was on a MED float en route to Beirut, per President Ronald Reagan's command; his unit stormed the beach of Grenada in a covert military operation. He did arrive in Beirut in time to rotate with the other Marines that were already there. He was the radio operator and among the last Americans to leave the soil of Beirut. As they lowered the American flag and moved away, the other side immediately raised their flag, signaling that they were now in control of the country. Shawn is the son of Pauline Caldwell and a single father of Tamashike and RaShawn, and grandfather of Yazemine, Rhyne and Noah.

Other Pottstown men and women serving in peacetime or in Vietnam, Germany, Korea Beirut or other duty stations:

- Ronnie Alexander
- Allen Allison
- Joseph Barringer
- James "Coo Bang" Barringer
- Ali Davis
- Whitfield Davis
- Harry Douglas
- Luke Douglas
- Joe Nathan Elmore
- Reginald Graham
- Bobby Hall
- Grayling Houston
- James Houston
- Larry Jackson
- William Kerns
- Chris G. Moore
- Clyde Moore, Jr.
- Ralph Moore
- Rose Moore
- Artis Moultry
- Michael Moultry
- Eric Neal
- Quan Neal
- Larry Patterson
- Louis Patterson
- Michael Pharr
- Regina Phillips
- Thomasina Phillips
- Walter Ross
- Rush Sherrill, Jr.
- Ernest Sloan
- Mary Sloan
- Stanley Sloan, Jr.
- Aaron Smith
- Billy Springs
- Garland Springs
- Gary Springs
- Roger Springs
- Pud Springs
- Skeet Spring
- Jerry Springs
- Barry Staton
- Robert Squarrels, Jr.
- Vernon Thompson
- Gregory Thompson
- Pee Wee Thompson
- Harrison S. Whitley
- William Whitley
- Robert Whitley

They Gave Their Lives

Lovette Sherrill, son of Verdie and Agusta Sherrill, was one of two men from Pottstown that died while serving in the Military. He was in the Air Force in 1957 when he drowned while in Texas. Daryl Clark, son of Betty and Peter Clark, Jr. died while on maneuvers.

Walter Harris had relatives in Pottstown. He enlisted in the Army when Vietnam was the destination for most new recruits. He had received orders to go. While training on maneuvers at Fort Benning, Georgia, he was on board a Huey helicopter when two of them collided. All were killed.

Walter Harris, Army soldier, was killed in 1965 when two Huey helicopters collided in Fort Benning, Georgia.

Airman, Lovette Sherrill, drowned in Texas' Red River in 1957.

Shawn Caldwell and fellow Marine in a bunker in Beirut

Mike Stewart and Shawn Caldwell about to board a bus for their first duty station at Jacksonville, NC.

Parris Island

Senator Jesse Helms

On the tarmac at Seymour Johnson AFB when the Desert Storm War ended

Paul Hicks was employed at Magla Mill before it moved to Mexico. Years later, it burned.

Betty Caldwell, Official Pen Pal, Volunteered for Duty During the Vietnam Conflict and Again During the Crisis in Beirut

Before "volunteering" as a "Pen Pal," my military experience was that of being the daughter, niece, cousin, sister, friend and aunt of men who had joined the Army, Air Force or Marines. During the Vietnam Conflict, I do remember my classmates, friends and brother who were stationed there. That is when I became a Pen Pal. The Charlotte News would list the names and addresses of all the local men and women who were on active duty there. I remember the nightly news with their count of the body bags. These bags contained the remains of humans. I did not fully understand the "why" of the war, the use of "Agent Orange" or the danger and seriousness of warfare, day by day.

During Vietnam, the media covered it with fewer graphics than what was done in Beirut. There they used the terms, "picking off our boys like flies." It was difficult for the Americans to distinguish just who the enemy was. The two groups fighting looked and dressed almost alike. They smiled and waved at you in the day time and you became their target at night.

The uncertainty of my love ones' well being was so unnerving that I took my portable TV to the office where I could ease my troubled mind by watching the news and sharing Shawn, Mike and Brad's letters/story with the girls at the office. We used cassette tapes most times instead of writing letters. Soon everyone in the building knew about me and "my Marines."

I was on "pen pal red alert duty" every day. Daily at lunch time I went to the park to pray for them. Mike and Brad called each other, "my ace in the hole." And I was their "pen pal, ace in the hole." So much so that when Brad was discharged from the Marines, instead of his going directly home to Chicago, he stopped by my job to meet me, the girls and folks at the office, personally. When Shawn and Mike were granted leave, they came by the office also.

From the onset of the two wars in 2001, I have not had to come out of retirement and resume my corresponding via pen pal letter writing. It's a new day and those in these wars can communicate by phone and actually see each other. So from an old school pen pal, I'll close by using the Marine motto, "Semper Fidelis!"

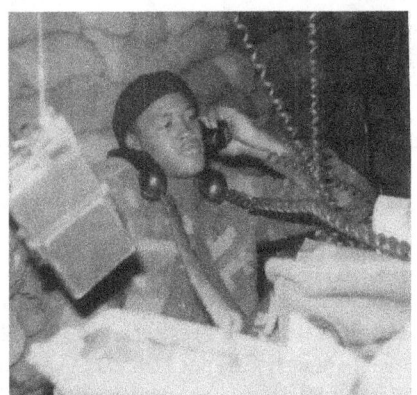

Shawn in 1984

Arthur L. Bradley

Marine buddies of Mike Stewart in uniform

Girls at my office, left to right, Gerry Wallace, Juanita Conger and Ratree Smith

Religious Activities and Functions

A Pottstown family's major religious activity was to attend church services on Sunday, prayer meeting on Wednesday nights and revival services in the spring and fall. Though treated as second class citizens, most believed that because we did not live in a perfect world, a time was needed to give back to God, the Creator of the Universe for all He had allowed us to accomplish. Each community had its own churches within walking distance. Inside Pottstown there were three, the United House of Prayer for all People, St. Phillips Baptist and Huntersville AME Zion (called Little Mission during that era). Other churches were Huntersville Presbyterian, now called New Friendship Presbyterian, Catawba Presbyterian, Hopewell AME Zion, Columbus Chapel, AME Zion, Jonahville AME Zion, Chapel Hill Baptist and Mt. Olive Baptist.

Bethesda AME Zion Church dissolved after many years as the older generation had passed on. At one time this church hosted the well-renowned August Bethesda Picnic. This was the church's "homecoming" and family members and friends would come home for this annual event.

The churches within Pottstown had the support of Mr. I. T. Graham, Torrence-Lytle's principal. Each summer Vacation Bible School was hosted by one of the area churches, he always approved their use of the school building and grounds.

******

Ms. Maggie Hicks, daughter of Reid and Esther Hicks, contains a wealth of knowledge about the history of Huntersville. All descendants of the enslaved did not live in Pottstown. They were scattered about in white communities as in the case of Gibson Park. Gibson Park is legendary as it was home to a white man named Scrubby Gibson. Now it is inhibited by blacks and is an adjacent to Vermillion Park.

A Presbyterian Church has existed uptown since it was started in 1886. Maggie has been a lifetime member. Years ago, the church housed a school where Reverend R. L. Moore taught students to read and write. At one time, there were two Presbyterian Churches in Huntersville, one black and one white. She laughs as she says their mail was never mixed up. It has been renamed New Friendship Presbyterian Church.

She is very proud that her dad was president of Huntersville's Colored School PTA for years while he worked 55 years at the Huntersville's Mill. He and his family lived in the front of the Rosenwald School and at one time he was responsible for making the fire in each of the four classrooms.

She ends her story by sharing that she does not know how segregation feels. "Living uptown in Huntersville," the stores only had one door and both races used it. Back then, we got along, the blacks and the whites.

Little Mission Huntersville AME Zion Church

St. Phillips Baptist Church

John Alexander and his wife's grave markers

The United House of Prayer

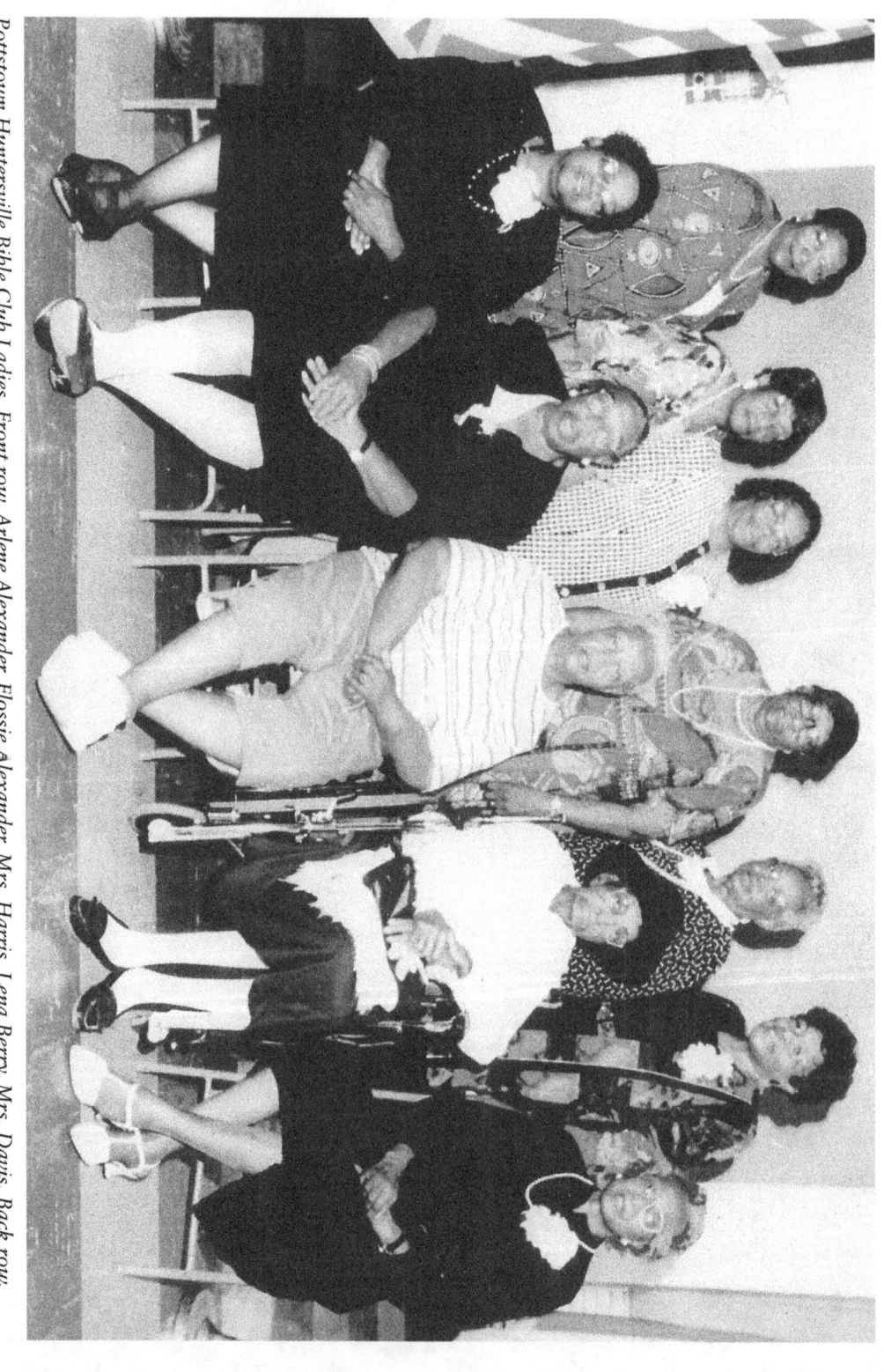

Pottstown Huntersville Bible Club Ladies. Front row, Arlene Alexander, Flossie Alexander, Mrs. Harris, Lena Berry, Mrs. Davis. Back row, Betty Phillips, Anna Barringer, Mrs. Dye, Emma Sloan, Mary Sherrill and Odessa Staton

BEE JAY ATTENDS MOUNT CARMEL BAPTIST CHURCH, WHEREVER YOU GO A MCBC MEMBER WILL BE THERE

Senior Pal, Frances Thomas

Musician and his son and my niece, Tam on a train ride

MCBC's third pastor, Leon C. Riddick (white hair)

Danny Mitchell, Associate Pastor at one time

Cultural Arts Committee, Velma Buxton, sisters, and Bee Jay Caldwell

Current Pastor, Casey Kimbrough and Bee Jay Caldwell

Recreation and Entertainment

From the time slavery ended and during the years of segregation (by law Negroes and whites had to be separated in all phases of life), Negro families had to find ways for recreation/socialization in their own communities. Many family members had moved away to make a better life for themselves, but wanted to come back every year. So the churches created "Camp Meetings." There were not many hotels* for Negroes, so the church allowed little "shacks" or "tents" to be built on the grounds of the church, and those visiting could bring their bedding and other comforts and live there for the week. There would be nightly church service, with singing and preaching under the arbor. Further away from the religious affairs would be vendors selling food, souvenirs and a jukebox where young and old would dance the day and night away.

Businesses were created to take care of social needs. Music was fundamental in almost all families. Someone in the family or block owned a radio, Victrola or record player. In the summer there were the outdoor picnics that took place rain or shine. Play the jukebox and dance to the music. Eat the twenty-five cent fish sandwiches, fifteen cent hot dogs and five cent drinks. What a life! Pottstown families made the best of life in the segregated south. It was truly a great time. With laws that separated the races, and with neighbors not having any more than you, parents protected their young from as much racism as possible, we never knew that we were thought of as poor outcasts.

Eventually, an entrepreneurial minded man or woman would open a place of business. The Brown sisters, Lena and Wealthy, noticed that when the Sherrills closed on Sundays, there was no place to buy even an ice cream cone. So they opened an ice cream shop called "Barringer and Berry's Place."

Someone else came up with the idea of a "juke joint" or dance hall where friends and family could get together and socialize. At these homes/settings, there would be a jukebox where one could put in a nickel, dime, or quarter and dance to the latest tunes that were played on the radio. The aroma of fish sandwiches could be smelled for blocks and became the calling card to gather the people. If you preferred a more private setting, the homes of Claude or John Gaston were available or at Evelyn's and "John Whit's."

Pottstown had a dance hall on Holbrooks Road and another one across the hill. In the 1950s, the Sherrill's added a large room to their grocery business. The "Store" became the place of choice to gather, play the jukebox and dance. Soon after it opened, a new resident in town opened the "Do Drop In" on Dellwood Drive.

After the Little School was closed and the students sent to Torrence-Lytle, the store became a community center where that all important "jukebox" played all the popular songs by Ruth Brown, Fats Domino and the Platters. This was the site of young people's universe on the weekends.

If and when you wanted something to drink, there were several beverages to choose from. Soda pop if you wanted a coke, ginger ale or orange drink. Beer was available but sold at certain times of the day because of the "blue laws." Home brew if you knew what ingredients to add to the water and not end up making a bomb. If you preferred the hard stuff, liquor was sold at the ABC Store in Charlotte, or you could seek out the local, undercover makers of white corn liquor, called "white lightning."

THE GREEN BOOK
(Help Solve Your Travel Problems, 1949)
by Wendell P. Alston, Special Rep Esso Standard Oil Co.)

Below is an excerpt from the introductory page from the Negro Motorist Green Book of 1949. Victor H. Green, a postal worker in Harlem, New York, who was also active in political affairs, started the Green Book in 1936 to let African Americans know where they would be welcomed when they traveled to different cities across the United States. **Many hotels and restaurants would not allow black people to use their facilities.**

Through the ages, men of all races have moved from place to place. Some to seek new lands, others to avoid persecution or intolerance and still for the sake of adventure.

Today, men of all races continue to move and for much the same reasons, though since the days of the foot travel and the ox-cart, they travel with much more convenience and comfort at a far greater speed.

For most travelers, whether they travel in modern high-speed motor cars, streamlined Diesel-powered trains, luxurious ocean liners or globe encircling planes, there are hotels of all sizes and classes, waiting and competing for their patronage. Pleasure resorts in the mountains and at the seashore beckon him. Roadside inns/cabins spot the highways and all are available if he has the price.

For some travelers however, many of these places are not available, even though they may be able to pay the price. Any traveler to whom they are not available, is thereby faced with many and sometimes difficult problems.

The Negro traveler's inconveniences are many and they are increasing because today so many more are traveling, individually and in groups.

This year for the annual convention of the largest Negro organization in the world, nine special trains in addition to those regularly scheduled, were required to transport more than fifty thousand of its members to a mid-western city. Several thousand more made the trip by car and some by plane.

Below are facilities in New Haven, Connecticut where travelers could refresh themselves. Tourist homes were private homes that would take in guests. Also listed were beauty salons, barbershops, garages/gas stations and night clubs where travelers could go for entertainment.

Hotel:	Phillis Wheatley – 108 Canal Street
Tourist Homes:	Dr. M. F. Allen – 65 Dixwell Avenue
	Mrs. C. Raone – 68 Dixwell Avenue
Restaurants:	Monterey – 267 Dixwell Avenue
	Belmonts – 156 Dixwell Avenue

Pottstown's Well-Known Sites

Espie Alexander Home on the National Register of historical sites

Berry and Barringer Place

Holbrooks Road Landfill changes its name often, and in 2016 it became Greenfield Waste.

Haircuts and Snowballs

There were no barber shops. So, my great Uncle Claude taught my Uncle June how to cut the neighbors' hair. No barber/beauty shop, Quincy Tucker and his wife, Sylvia, opened a shop they shared. Soon Wilma Burton opened her own beauty shop.

If you needed gas, Pigg's gas and service station was just a few steps across the rail road tracks that divided the Negroes from the whites.

What fun we had when Stanley Sloan, his wife, Emma and family learned how to make ten cent snowballs and take twenty-five cent pictures. We owe a sincere "thank you" to them for those unselfish acts. And did we not enjoy the popcorn that June Kerns sold at picnics for a nickel or a dime? And there would definitely be fish, hot dogs and drinks. Oooh, how good the food tasted as you stood and fought the flies to eat it.

Take Us Out to the Ball Game

In pursuit of happiness, several men played baseball, the game of choice for men during the 1940s and 50s. Chris Springs was the manager of the men's ball team. Many a Saturday afternoon, families would gather at a ball field in one of the little Negro communities. Either at Long Creek by Catawba Presbyterian Church, or Lytle Grove at Columbus Chapel AME Zion Church or at Smithfield at the Rosenwald School turned into a community center. And most certainly the ball field at Torrence-Lytle High School. Among the best players were, John Lee Caldwell, Bart Jetton, and Tom Johnson. Isaac Harris was sought after by local white teams and was the better known of them all.

Clyde Moore managed and sponsored the youth baseball team. Every one was impressed when he gave them red baseball caps. My brother, Pete, liked his so much that he only removed it after he got into bed at night.

Halloween Tricks (or Rites of Passage)

Every Halloween there seemed to have been a ritual that the men, boys and some girls participated in. These nocturnal (night time) tricksters would move a family's outhouse and place it on the steps of the school. And Mr. Otha's wagon would be pulled away from the barn to a new location. One night these pranksters got a surprise. He was waiting for them with his shotgun.

The buckshot did not hurt any one, but it did make them run for their lives.

A Dark Side of Pottstown's Life

As in most Negro communities, at times there would be issues with the sin-filled side of life. There was domestic violence and wives, Ossie Lee Lynch, Cat Alexander and Mildred Morrison were killed. Sporadically, one man would take the law into his own hands and take the life of another. The names of some victims included: David Alexander's brother, Isaac Kerns, Harry Haines, Ida Howard, James Alexander, Mac Doodle Davis, Fonzo Wilson, Annie Belle Sloan and Jab Bo Sloan. When we were in the sixth grade my classmate, William Potts, died of a mysterious death.

Individuals Living in Pottstown

Parks Ross, son of WWI veteran, Cleo Ross

Artis Moultry

Le Andy Houston and Mot Sherrill (brothers-in-law)

Alexander Henderson and wife, Frankie

James "Pete" Caldwell

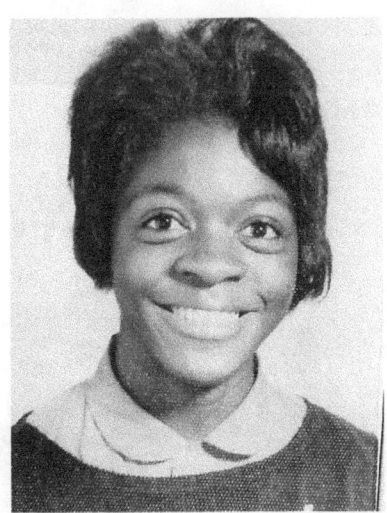

Harriet Gaston

Garland Springs

Teretha Connor and daughter, Dorothy

*Golden Peacemaker,
Annie Blaire Hughey*

Teretha Connor, a Pottstown mother

TLHS classmates of 1962

*Former teacher, Esther Johnson at
HCDA's annual spring festival*

A woman stands in front of two outdoor toilets.

Bessie Kimble, neice, Montez Shankle's great grandmother

Gayland Sherrill at his North Meck Graduation

Pauline, Hazel and Diane in New Orleans

Cousin Karen Sherrill and her daughter

Chapel Hill's former pastor, Kay F. Gamble, wife, Agnes and his family: Tommy, Saundra and her husband, and Myra.

Cousin, Gladys Caison Dixon

Mrs. Iabelle Hudson, and nephew, Sam Barringer shared with me in telling the Pottstown story.

Isabelle's niece, Annie, was always ready to care for her auntie.

TLHS Class of 1965 members, Rush Sherrill, Jimmy (Willie) Nance and Latra Jetton

Pauline and Patrick Carr after cutting the grass

James "Bo" Howard and Johnny Leazer

Shorty Sherrill, Pauline and Burnice Anderson

Schoolmate and friend, Hershey Gabriel

Huntersville Community Development Association's 1999 Spring Festival

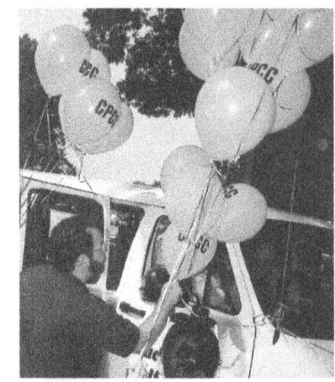

Mount Olive Baptist and Hopewell AME Zion Churches

Tyla Smith was a queen in the parade

Pauline Caldwell and another student represented CPCC

Mayor Randy Quillen and Tim Bresslyn led the parade

Shirley Caldwell represented Chapel Hill Church in the parade

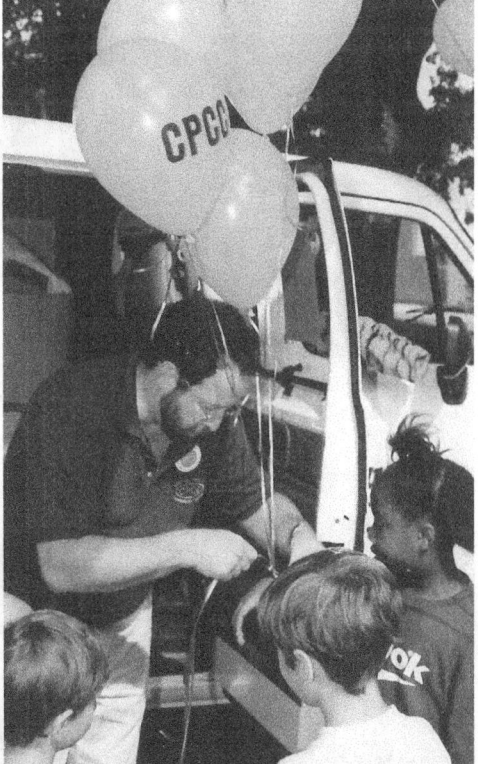
Student Life Coordinator, Barry, represented North Campus

School mates at the Blue and Gold Dance: Geneva Neal, Willie Grissom, Georgia Leazer, Claudine Rhyne

Family friends, Ralph and Anne Richardson

The Love family, Ken, Cynthia and Derrick at LaToya's Debutant Ball

Cynthia Love and son, Derrick

My co-worker, Ratree Smith's daughter, Erica at her graduation

The 26th Annual
HCDA Spring Festival
and
Pre-Juneteenth Program

Saturday, June 1, 2002
Torrence-Lytle Center
310 Dellwood Drive
Huntersville, NC 28078
2:00 PM

Program

Bee Jay Caldwell, Mistress of Ceremony

Invocation/Greetings

The Occasion
   A Juneteenth Celebration
   Remembering our Rosenwald Schools
   A Walk-Through Art Exhibit

Musical Selection

The History of Juneteenth
   Re-enactment of General Order
   Number 3

Musical Selection

The History of Rosenwald Schools   Mrs. Juanita Moore
   Huntersville, NC

Story of a Rosenwald Day Celebration

Musical Selection

Use of Rosenwald Schools Today   Mr. George Wallace
   Grier Heights Foundation
   Charlotte, NC

Entertainment   *Youth of Greater Hopewell AME Zion Church*

Artist of the Day   Mr. Cameron Johnson
   Rising Senior
   East Carolina University

Recognitions

Reflections/Remarks

Closing Prayer and Grace

Reception immediately following the program

"Juneteenth and The Rosenwald Legend live."

History of Juneteenth

What is Juneteenth? Juneteenth is the oldest known celebration of the ending of slavery. Dating back to 1865, it was June 19th that the Union soldiers, led by Major General Gordon Granger, landed at Galveston, Texas with news that the war had ended and that all slaves were now free. Note that this was two and a half years after President Lincoln's Emancipation Proclamation — which had become official January 1, 1863. The Emancipation Proclamation had little impact on the Texans due to the minimal number of Union troops to enforce the new Executive order. However, with the surrender of General Lee in April 1865, and the arrival of General Granger's regiment, the forces were finally strong enough to influence and overcome the resistance.

Later attempts to explain the two and a half year delay in the receipt of this important news have yielded several versions that have been handed down through the years. Often told is the story of a messenger who was murdered on his way to Texas with the news of freedom. Another, is that the news was deliberately withheld by the slave masters to maintain the labor force on the plantations. And still another, is that federal troops actually waited for the slave owners to reap the benefits of one last cotton harvest before going to Texas to enforce the Emancipation Proclamation. All or neither could be true. For whatever reason, conditions in Texas remained status quo well beyond what was statutory.

General Order Number 3

One of General Granger's first orders of business was to read to the people of Texas, General Order Number 3 which began most significantly with: "The people of Texas are informed that in accordance with a Proclamation from the Executive of the United States, all slaves are free. This involves an absolute equality of rights and rights of property between former masters and slaves, and the connection heretofore existing between them becomes that between employer and free laborer."

In Recognition of My Ancestors
by Betty Jane "Bee Jay" Caldwell

The First Generation

Our history begins in the 1820s with the birth of our oldest ancestor, Eli Alexander in the Hopewell community. He was brought up on a plantation owned by Alexanders from Ireland, who were doctors by profession. He was never a slave, wore his hair long and could read and write because his mother was white. Eli's first wife was a slave named Caroline who was a mixture of African, white and Indian ancestry. They had one son, John and two daughters, Anna and Eliza. After Caroline died, Eli married his second wife, Matilda. They lived in Mooresville, rented rooms to local preachers and were instrumental in the formation of Watkins Chapel AME Zion Church. At this church, everyone sat according to his color — the lighter you were the closer to the front you sat. Eli was well-to-do and traveled in a horse and carriage. The late Les Frazier and other Negroes worked for him in the early 1900s. He died in 1918. (He may have had two other sons, Elmo and Henry, but that has been lost to time. As told to Bee Jay in 1982 by Mr. Price Caldwell).

The Second Generation

John Alexander was the better known of the three Alexander siblings and was called "a big shot" by all who knew him. Born in 1859, he was the only blacksmith in Huntersville at one time, and lived "uptown" on Church Street in a two story house. His shop was along side of Holbrooks Delivery Stable. He was married but we don't have his wife's name. They adopted two daughters and their names are lost to time also. He died before his dad in 1918 and left silver, furniture and twenty-five acres of land to his sisters. At his funeral, he was buried in a black casket that many had never seen before. (Most people in those days were buried in a wood coffin, shaped smaller at the foot and wider at the top.) Taxes were not paid on the property and the land was purchased for $300 by Bruce Smith in the 1940s. The property was bounded by properties owned by Otha Potts, Cleo Ross, Scruby Gibson, Glen Lane and Raleigh White.

Both Liza and Anna were midwives. Liza married Frank Rhyne from Fisher Town in Cabarrus County.

Anna, my great, great grandmother was born two years after the Civil War in 1867. For over sixty years, "Aunt Anna" brought many babies, both black and white into the world. When the time came for the baby to be born, the husband would come for Anna. She would pick up her little black bag, and remain in their home until the baby was born. She was not always paid in cash. Sometimes she was given chickens, eggs, meat from the smoke house or butter.

Anna married Andrew "Andy" Brown and as a couple, they enjoyed the luxury of a Franklin car. Andy suffered from "the dropsy" and passed away. Today we know that he suffered from heart disease. They were blessed with six children, John, Will, Pearl, Jane, Anne and Matilda.

The Third Generation

My great grandmother, Matilda, was their youngest daughter. She did not have a birth certificate, so we computed her age using her age at the time of her marriage. When she was approximately fourteen years old, she eloped and married Sephus Turner. Their first child, Charlie died. Their second child, Annie Mae, was born in 1900. We determined that Matilda was approximately seventeen years old in 1900. Subtract seventeen from 1900 and her approximate birth year is 1883 or 1884. Sephus was one of Reverend and Mrs. Sam Turner's nine children: John, Will, Abe, Andy, Dee (of Wheeling, West Virginia) Mary, Sally Sloop and Ila.

Sephus and Matilda "Tilla" had thirteen children. One died during childbirth and Charlie died at twelve months old. The boys were James, DeWitt and Claude. They married but never fathered children. The girls were Annie Mae, Pearl, Carrie, Eva, Verdie, Hallie, Fannie, and Margaret. Sephus died from a gun shot wound leaving Tillie with several children. She moved frequently from one sharecropper's farm to another. Annie Mae and Verdie married and had large families. When the children became teenagers, they left home and went North for a better life.

The Fourth Generation

My grandmother, Pearl, was not so lucky. She died of consumption in 1929 or 1930 leaving her two daughters, Mamie and Shirley, orphaned. Tillie, being the devoted grandmother she was, took in her granddaughters and reared them as though they were her own children. That is why five generations called Tillie, "Momma."

The Fifth Generation

My mother, Shirley, met her future husband while working at the TB Sanitarium in Huntersville. She married Spurgeon Willis Caldwell and they were parents to Shirley, "Sugar Pea," Pete, Betty and Pauline. Both always worked out of the home. As a result, great grandmother, Tillie, lived with them and provided child care for the family. After the birth of their youngest daughter, Pauline, Shirley worked continuously at the same site at the TB hospital that changed names often, and retired as a cook in 1987.

Paternal Side of the Family

Spurgeon was the "knee baby" born to Hessie Watts and Lawrence Caldwell and was the grandson of Henry and Harriett Watts. They made their home in Lemly, North Carolina, a little community near HWY #73 and Beatties Ford Road. When Hessie died, her oldest daughter, Roberta became their surrogate mother. Their sister, Queenie Madge, died as a teenager. Clifford, the youngest of the family, never knew his mother. His brothers were Jethro, James, and Spurgeon. Their dad married Plume Johnson and their children were John Lee, Craven and Ruth. She passed away and he remarried and they have a daughter, Joanne "Toosie" who lives in Cornelius, North Carolina. The 1910 census shows that Lawrence was fourteen when they lived with an uncle named Mose Caldwell. In the 1940s, he worked at Huntersville's cotton mill as a supervisor of the Negro men who worked loading cotton onto the trains. Spurgeon passed away in 1975 at 52 years old.

The Sixth Generation

The sixth generations of Alexanders have evolved from the Browns, the Turners to the Caldwells. The Caldwell "chaps" are baby boomers, Sugar Pea (deceased) Pete, Betty and Pauline. Sugar Pea married James "Bo" Howard and blessed Spurgeon and Shirley with grandchildren; Avery, Nette and Terry, lovingly called, "the Bug Heads." Pere is dad to Montez and he married Anne Dardgen and they are proud parents of Tony and April, a Duke University graduate. Pauline is mom to her one and only son, Shawn, grandmother to Tamshieka and Ra Shawn and great grandmother to Yazemine, Rhyne and Noah. Last but not least is Betty, better known as Bee Jay, and she has no children.

The Seventh Generation

Neither of the Howard children had children. With Avery deceased, and Terry incarcerated, and Nette recuperating from a stroke, there is not much hope for them to start families. After the preceding generations, the millennials are hard to keep up with. They are Montez's children,

Adrian, Marcus, and Tomeka, Shawn's daughter, Tamasheika "Tam" and son, RaShawn, and Tony's daughter, Dominique.

The Eighth Generation

As of 2016, this is the very last generation of all because each descendant is less than ten years old. Perhaps in ten or fifteen years the ninth generation will come into being. This eighth generation chooses not to have close ties with family. Adrian has children, but I'm not sure of the number. To our knowledge Marcus does not have any children. Tomeka has a son and daughter. RaShawn has three children, two daughters, Yazemine and Rhyne and a son, Noah.

My Story Began on the Way to School

On the way to school as I walked from one side of Pottstown to the other each morning, I took careful note of my surroundings.

The very first thing I had to do was to get up enough nerve to walk under the worm trees. I was, and still am, afraid of the worms that come out on oak trees in the fall.

Then I had to carefully descend down the hill with tree roots going every which way to get to the "Little School," across the hill.

At the bottom of the hill, I stopped to admire the water coming up out of the spring and then jumped the creek made by it.

Climbing up the hill was not nearly as bad as coming down.

I would always stop and look at the direction the road took. Seems like some of the houses were in the road, and it veered just enough so that a car could pass by and not hit it.

The road had ruts in it where rainwater had carved out its own path. Some houses had never been painted and others had paint peeling off them.

Family members sat on the porch and called out a greeting to me. Others would come to the door to see who was passing by. And some just may call out to me from a window. Every one was so friendly that there was nothing to fear. On either side of the hill, the only person with a dog that would bite was Mr. Henry Pharr.

My favorite place to stop was at Mr. Dee Alexander's house. He was a little old man who did not mind if I stopped by every day for a short visit. I had never seen so many flowers in one place before. He was so kind and his little house was so inviting. He would have to tell me when it was time to head to school, or be late. I was so close that I could run the rest of the way, cut through the different yards, walk through the narrow road where the trees grew together, forming something like a tunnel, and get to school on time. In first grade, I was Mrs. Streater's pet student.

In third grade, I was given the responsibility of taking the attendance report to the principal's office at the high school.

I loved school even after I got in trouble taking up for my cousin, William. He was being "picked on" by DeWitt. I used my umbrella to help him understand that it was not a good idea to mess with my cousin or any of us.

From the time I was assigned to the new addition at Torrence-Lytle, I would play in our back yard on the "look out" for a teacher's car on the bus ramp. If I saw one, I would walk out of our yard through the neighbor's yard to get to the bus ramp and ask that teacher if I could assist her in any way. Soon, I became a "fixture" there.

I graduated in June 1964, attended Southeaster Business College for a quarter and returned home to enroll in Johnson C. Smith University. Of course I walked over to the school to greet the principal and teachers. I was not aware of an opening in the library. I had been a library assistant all during high school. When I shared my plans with Mrs. Johnson about enrolling at JCSU, she asked if I would be interested in working with her starting in January. For sure I said ,"Yes." We consulted Mr. Graham, and he approved. He instructed me to go to the schoolboard and apply and I got the job.

Nothing Just Happens — Destiny Takes Its Own Course

My story could not be written unless I shared the stories of those in my Pottstown community. These individuals changed the rest of my life. God has a string on my life — He's the puppeteer, I'm the puppet. The people He placed in my life were "props" there for a reason and a season to help me on "my destiny journey."

THE CALDWELL FAMILY

Shirley and Betty

Spurgeon, Shirley, Pete, Betty, Pauline and Shawn

James "Pete"

Shirley "Sugar Pea"

Spurgie and Shack

Shirley at work

Pauline

Our Dad Passed Away, Leaving my Mother, Shirley, to Raise the Children. She Passed in 2007.

Shirley

Shirley

Birthday money

Shirley

Shirley

Shirley and Betty

Betty, Shirley and Pete

Shawn and his dogs

Shirley, Betty and Pauline

Shirley, great grand, Tomeka and friend

Family friends, Hallie, Rena and Shirley

Shirley's sister-in-law, Ethel Caldwell

Sisters, Mamie and Shirley, daughter, Barbara and grandson, Rondale

Cousin Ruth and her cousin

Shirley, Pauline, Shawn and his daughter and son, RaShawn

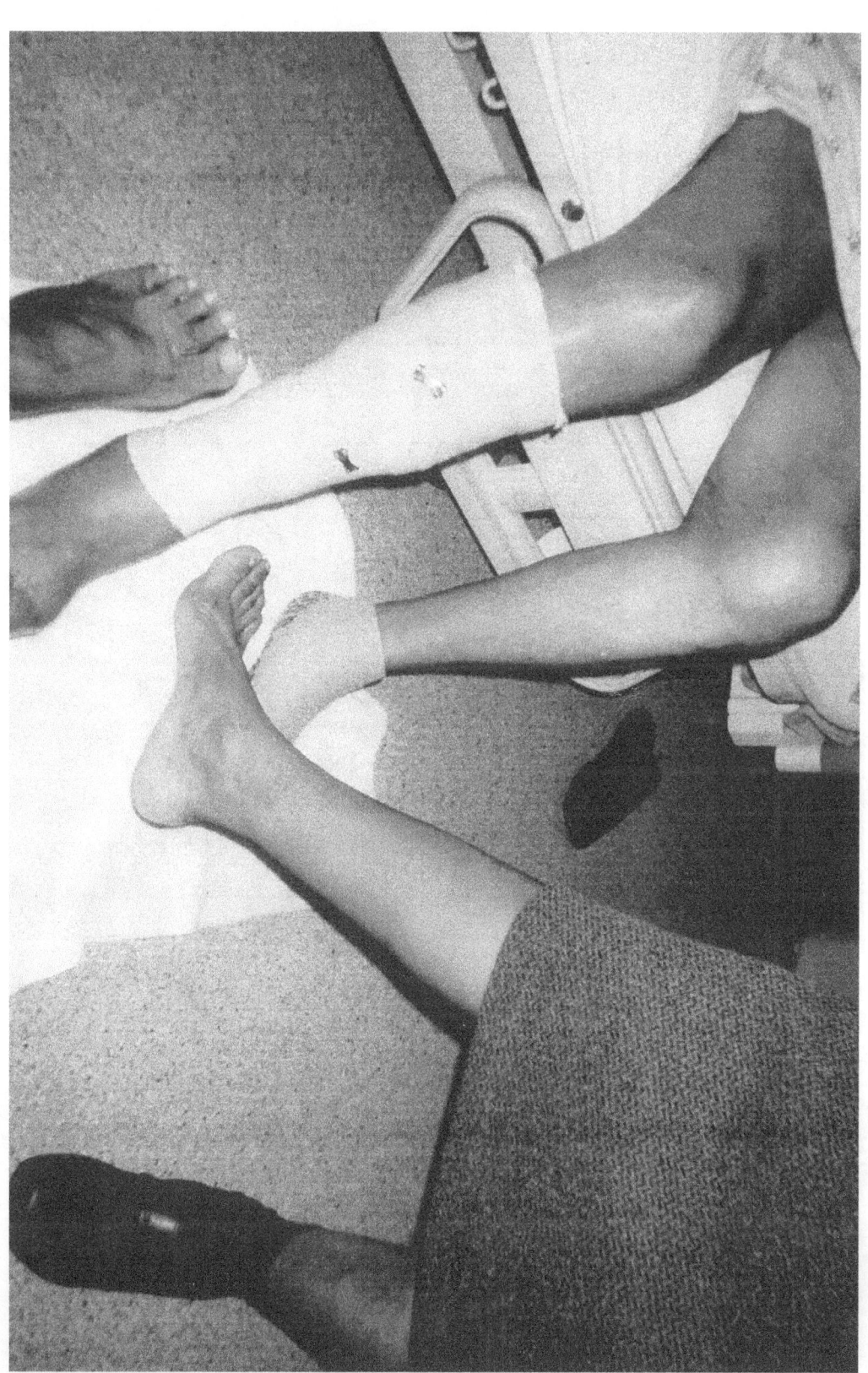

Picture of our legs before Shirley lost hers

Sugar Pea's Family; Avery, Sugar Pea and Nette and Terry

PETE, HIS WIFE AND FAMILY

Tony and April

Pete's oldest daughter, Montez, her son, Adrian and Pete's daughter, April

Pete and Anne

Bessie with her husband and their nephew, Tony

Pete's granddaughter, Tomeka

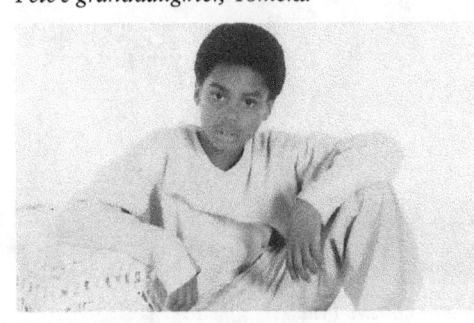

Pete's grandson, Marcus

Anne

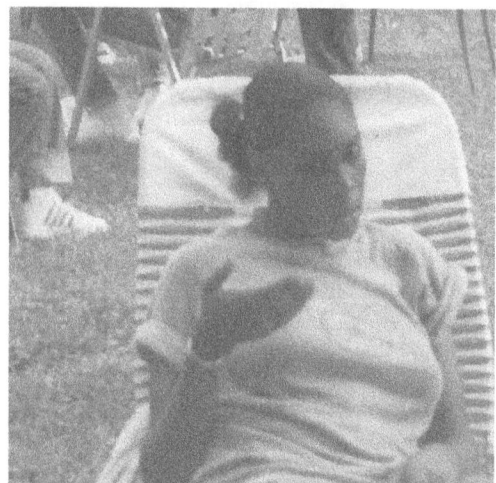

Pete's daughter, Montez

Adrian, Marcus and Tomeka at the zoo

Adrian, Marcus and Tomeka at the Tweetsie Railroad

Tomeka

Tomeka and cousin Tyla

BETTY THROUGH THE YEARS

Betty at the beach with Pauline, Pearl and Gloria

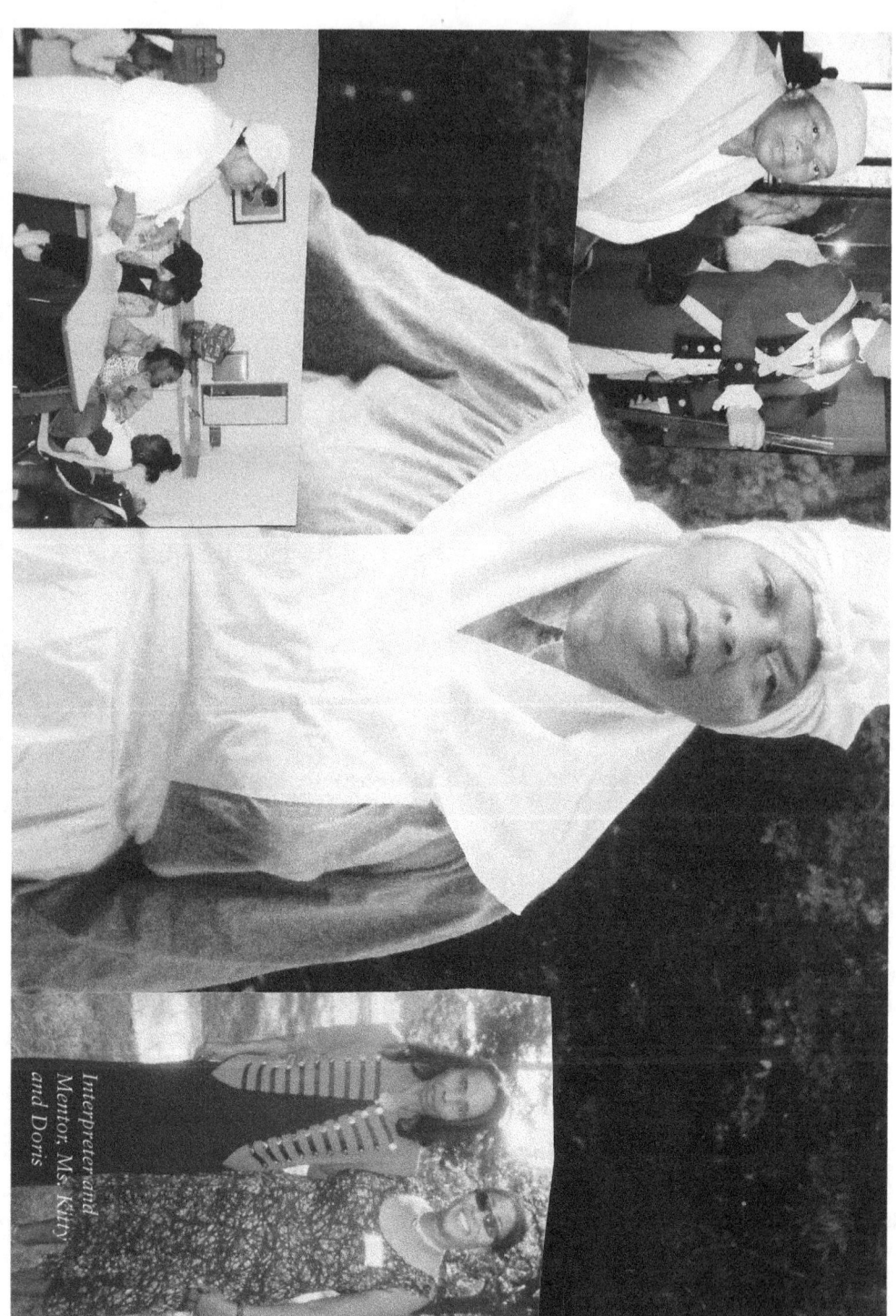

Betty is now Bee Jay. She is a female interpreter, who dresses as an enslaved person and speaks as though she is that person at re-enactments.

Interpreter and Mentor, Ms. Kitty and Doris

Pauline's Family

Pauline and son, Shawn

Pauline with grandson, RaShawn

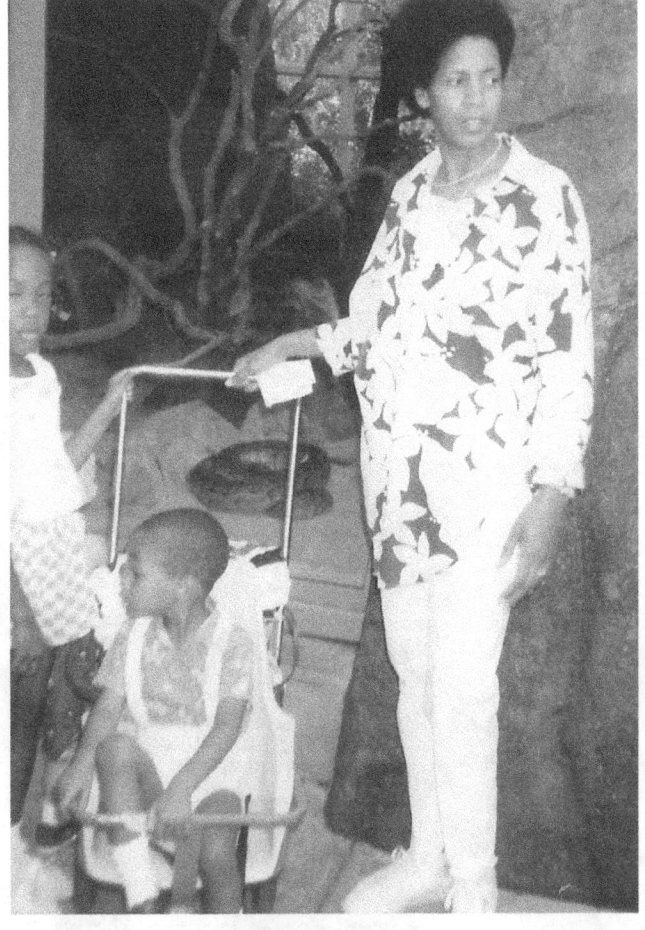

Pauline with grandson, RaShawn and granddaughter, Tamashikka

Pauline and Pete

Pauline and granddaughter, Tamashikka

Pauline

Pauline's home

Pauline and Shawn

Pauline and Shawn

Pauline at Duke University

Pauline's friend, Vivian

Pauline

Pauline and cousin Pearl

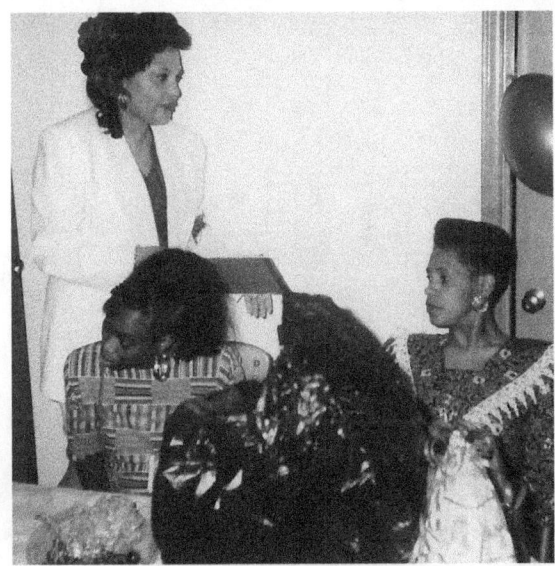
Pauline and cousin Pearl

Pauline and cousin Bob

Pauline with Vivian, Shawn, her instructor and Rose

Pauline was an honor graduate from CPCC.

Pauline, Shawn and Tanya and Curtis Hughes

The Bug Heads are my Parents' Grandchildren

The Bug Heads on my first car, a 1964 Malibu

Betty with Shawn, Vern and Dale

Our dad's 1955 Chevrolet

The Bug Heads on the steps of my apartment

The Bug Heads, our mother's names for her grands. Avery, Nette, Terry and Shawn seen in the backyard of our house

Shawn's birthday, his mom and cousin, Gayland

GRANDDAUGHTER TAM

Pauline's oldest grand, Tamasheika, a 2004 Barber Scotia graduate

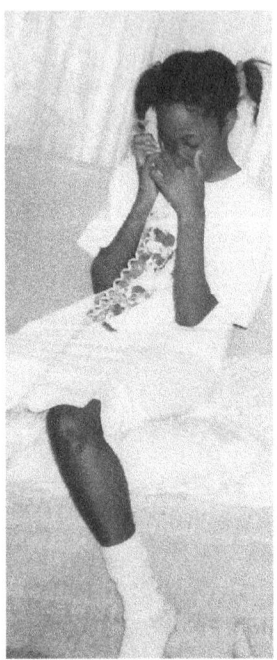

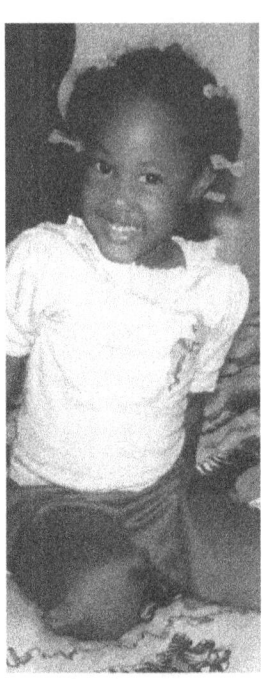

Tam, Shawn's daughter was a great source of joy while he was in Beirut.

Grandson Shawn, Great Grandson, RaShawn, Great-Great Granddaughter, Yazemine

RaShawn and his daughter, Yazemine

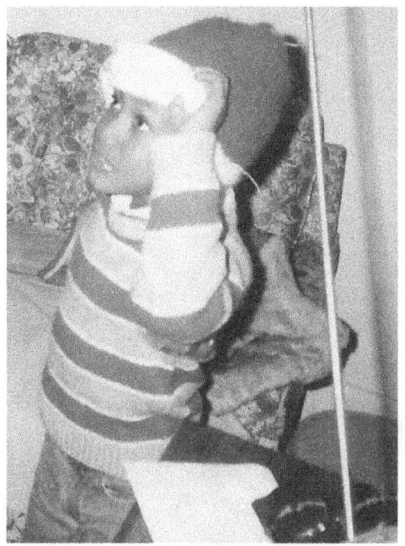

RaShawn is Shawn's son

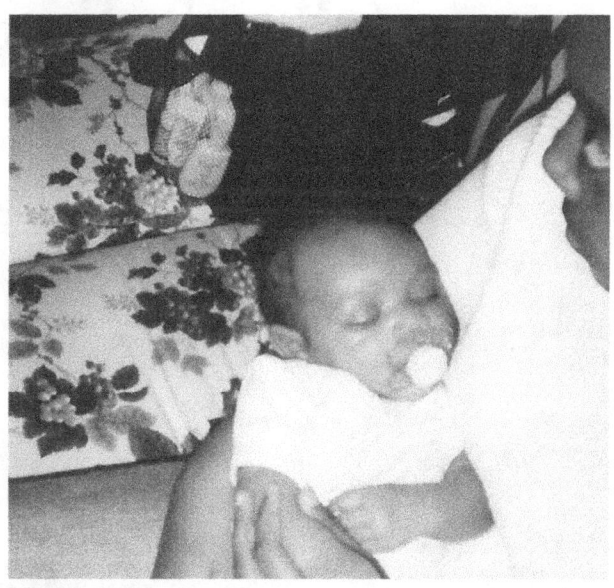

RaShawn on the back of my truck

RaShawn and Yazemine

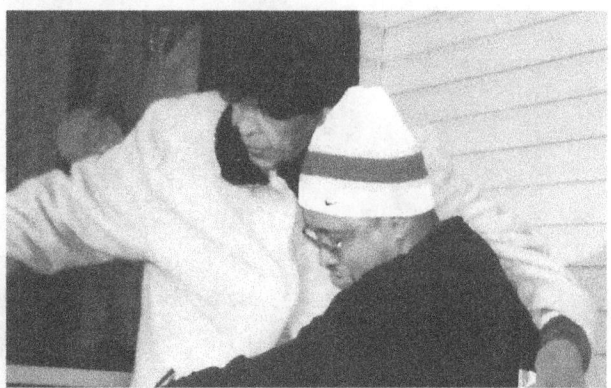

Moth Moth and RaShawn

Moth Moth and grandson, Shawn

THE KERNS FAMILY

Aunt Mamie

Uncle William Kerns, Sr.

Mamie at work

William

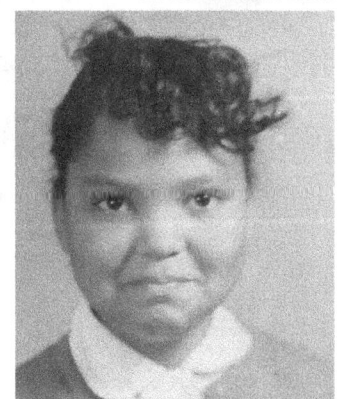
Carolyn

Grandson, Chad and his prom date

The Kerns' children, Bob, Pearl, William, Carolyn and Diane

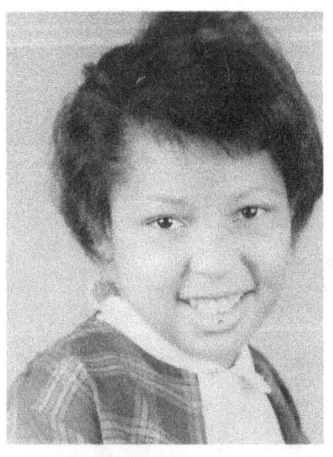
Diane

Diane and daughter, Camille

THE KERNS' GRANDCHILDREN AND GREAT GRANDS

Carolyn and husband, Slick

Barbara and Furman Smith

Carolyn's and son, Chad

Dale Smith

Carolyn's wedding

Gerald Smith

Granddaughters, Tyla and Tressa Smith

AUNTS, UNCLES AND COUSINS

2009's New Jersey visit to Aunt Hallie's

Cousin Ruby and daughter, Edna

Aunt Hallie's December 26th birthday

Claude Turner and wife, Annie Whitley

Cousin Ruby and son, Osmond and wife, Diane

Pauline on a cruise

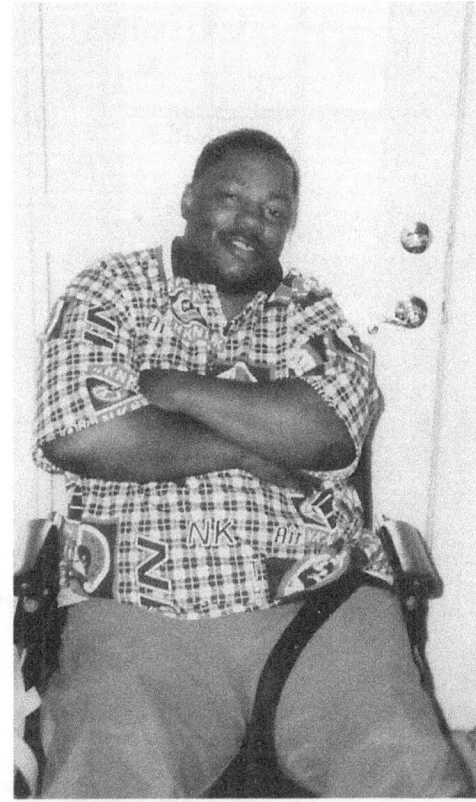
Avery Howard

Aunt Hallie on Pauline's porch

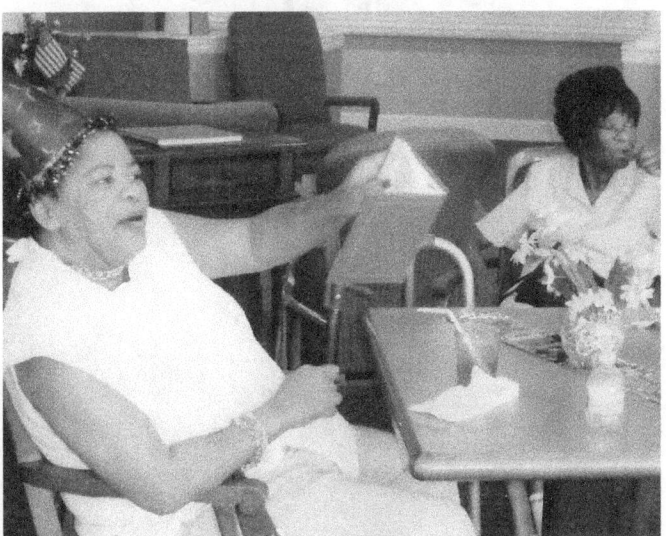
Nette and Aunt Hallie at the Oaks

COUSINS AND MORE COUSINS

Bob, Runt, Calvin, Edna and their family from Virginia

Betty, Cousin Harold and a friend at Myrtle Beach, SC

Cousin Anthony Sherrill, his wife, Angel and family

Betty and cousin Edna

Bob, Runt and Calvin

Bob and Shondale

Our first cousins, Bob, Pearl, William and Diane

Julius Rosenwald's grandson visited Billingsville Rosenwald School. We are so proud of what his grandfather did for Negroes. We did not know how to react.

Bee Jay participating in a CNA clinical in Mooresville, NC

Bee Jay at work at CPCC North Campus

The Sherrill Cousins

Margaret

Vivian

Isaac

Hanover

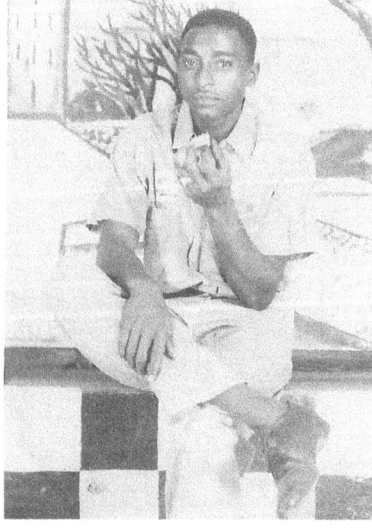
Gus Nathaniel   *"Mot"*

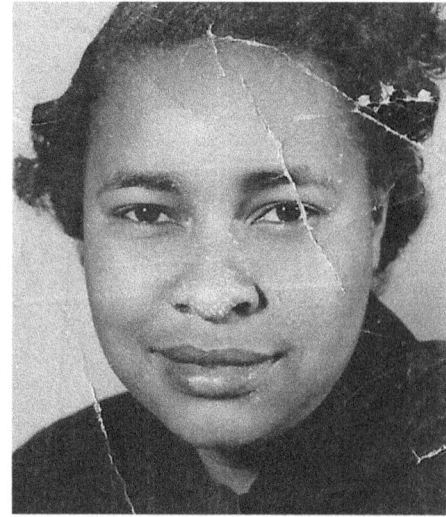
Faye

Isaac and Faye's husband, Barney

Hanover and Joanne Sloan

Everett

Grant on the Green, Betty's Haven since 1993

The house where supernatural events between me and my deceased sister, Sugar Pea, occurred.

Bee Jay's 1998 Mazda Truck

Bee Jay's mentor, Dr. Ayabba Bey and cousin, Sandra

Bee Jay and her supervisor, Hazel and Aunt Hallie at the Bowling Lane in Huntersville, NC

Family and friends in Boston, Massachusetts: Aunt Edna, her daughter, Helen, Hazel and Carolyn

Epilogue

In Pottstown in 2016, not much has changed since the 1940s. But a few years ago, new residents moved into the un-incorporated area that borders Pottstown. Much to our surprise, we learned that it is not against the law to discharge a firearm here. One resident from Michigan learned this and built a gun range in his backyard. Holbrooks Road is less than 300 feet away from its home base. When the police were called, neighbors were informed that he was within his legal rights, and there was nothing they could do about it. But to those of us who have lived here all of our lives, waking up Christmas morning, or any other time of day, to automatic gunfire like we are in a war zone is hard to adjust to. When another new resident hears this gunfire, he fires back and empties his semi-automatic weapon. What can neighbors do? Nothing! They are within their rights.

In 2016, there is no store to purchase any goods. Hopefully that will change and soon. Mecklenburg County Commissioners are spending 1.3 million dollars to restore Waymer Center (the C. DeWitt Bradford Gym) to its original condition. The Historic Landmarks Commission's plans to renovate the Torrence-Lytle classrooms signals that change is on the way. Already listed as "Prime Property," this will put Pottstown in the public's eye to a greater degree. This is not a bad thing. It will give home owners/citizens a unique opportunity to make their property as attractive as possible. *Not to sell,* but for them to *keep* and continue to live here. If you believe that the time is *now* for a much needed change for our Pottstown community, please support these efforts and pray that with God, people and government working together, a positive transformation can take place and the area not fall victim to gentrification.

Biography of Betty Jane "Bee Jay" Caldwell

Working under the name of Betty Caldwell, she retired in 1994 from Charlotte-Mecklenburg Schools, and entered into a venture where-in she had to make presentations. Bee Jay found this difficult, so her up-line manager suggested that she get a name that empowered her. A person called her home seeking a "B.J. Caldwell" that was not her. She liked the name, B.J. It did empower her! She made a decision to work in the new company as Bee Jay, and has ever since.

As Bee Jay, she has been attached to former slave plantations, now called "living farms" where she is a costumed interpreter, speaking in the first person as one of the Africans enslaved there. Her responsibility is to tell the story of those who did not have a voice to share their own.

She enjoys sharing stories of how the "Spirit of the Ancestors" is always present in her life. She is surprised sometimes when the Spirit shows up and she must re-invent herself, as it did recently when she was compelled to write the book, "Historic Pottstown Families in Stories and Photos."

Having been discriminated against often in her life, one of her favorite sayings is, "treat others as you wish to be treated." The legacy she wishes to leave behind is "that I was a fair team player."

www.ingramcontent.com/pod-product-compliance
Lightning Source LLC
Chambersburg PA
CBHW080455170426
43196CB00016B/2814